# HEALING
# THOUGHTS

# HEALING THOUGHTS

### Revised Edition

## Julia Neal Sykes

*Julia Neal Sykes*

## KAMKYI BOOKS
### Bronx, New York

REVISED EDITION

Published by Kamkyi Books
939 East 156 Street, Bronx, New York 10455

Manufactured in the United States of America
ISBN: 0-967503-0-8

Library of Congress Control Number: 00-131077

Cover art by Carmen Hall

Edited by Claire C. Harris

In Memory of My Husband
The Late Rev. R. B. Sykes
and My  Cat, Fluffy

Dedicated to

My Son: James E. Neal
Grandchildren: Kendra and Jared Neal
And All Descendants of
the late Mary and Clarence Neal

# Contents

## Feelings

# Friendship

# Love and Passion

# Nature

# People

# Spiritual Inspiration

## Holidays

# Foreword

Many people have the misguided idea that their minds become dull in their senior years and there are no new skills left for them to pursue. But that is far from being true in most instances. As we grow older there is still a vast area of untapped resources in the brain. We only need some type of motivation to bring those new skills to the surface. That motivation may be a sudden tragedy, grief, illness, loneliness or any other unwanted intruder in our lives.

At sixty-four, I found myself faced with grief and loneliness and discovered that I had a hidden gift of writing poetry. My first grief was the loss of my cat, "Fluffy," when some dogs killed her. We'd had her seventeen years and she was like a member of the family. I made a scrapbook in her memory and wrote a poem about the love she'd brought to us.

My niece, Valada Tinnin, read it and was so impressed with it she couldn't believe I wrote it. That inspired me to enter it in a poetry contest and it won honorable mention.

During the last days of my husband's illness with cancer, I was faced with more grief and turmoil of the worst kind. It was devastating to helplessly sit by and watch him waste away from a 192-pound active person to an extremely fragile man.

I had to do something, so I turned my thoughts inward to the dark corners of my soul and began to express my feelings by writing poetry again. I saw life from a new perspective. Things that I had taken for granted took on a new dimension. The little things of nature were seen from a different viewpoint. Everything was precious and special. Living each day, one at a time, was special.

When my husband was too sick for me to communicate with him, I sat by his bed and wrote poetry.

After his death I was filled with grief and loneliness, miles away from all of my relatives. Again, I turned to my writing to fill the void and found inner peace and a profound healing for my grief. Thus the title of this book, *Healing Thoughts*, was born.

## Acknowledgments

Heartfelt thanks to my family, friends, and members of Bear Creek Missionary Baptist Association for their financial support. Also to typists Ruth Lane and Olga Musgrow.

# YES, I CAN

## The Saga of My Life

Each time I see an ant hill – the neatly formed mound
of dirt around a perfectly constructed hole – I see a
miracle.

How these tiny creatures achieve this feat by working
together – bringing out one little particle of dirt
at a time – serves as inspiration.

When the cares on life's highway get me down.
When the roadblocks of failure and the little orange
construction barrels of rejection and defeat get in
my way. Detours of broken promises on every side.

Bridges of determination – out up ahead. With a long
line of impatient motorists out to get me, honking
their horns behind me. I can't turn back, or go
forward. Ready to give up – I think about that
little ant and loudly proclaim,
"Yes I Can! I can find a way to go forward!"

Taking a quick stroll back over the three score and
ten years I've lived this life – I see it unfolding
like a rose blossom – petal by Petal. Emitting the
sweet smell of triumph and success in a multitude of
undertakings.

When I became an unwed mother, society at that time,
like the ranchers branded their cattle, branded me.
Circumstances and public sentiment told me I was a
"nobody". I was down – so stay down!

As a baby chick pecks its way out of the egg shell
in search of life – I too, said "Yes, I Can!
I can claw my way out of this unwed mother syndrome
and find a new life".

Turning my thoughts inward to the core of my being –
started – one day at a time. I hem the curtain of
each day with hope to keep out the darkness of the
night of despair.

Allowing a candle of confidence to kindle the flame
of courage – igniting my determination to forge ahead.
"Yes, I can! I can make tomorrow better!
I can make my world better!"

Leaving the outskirts of my memories – other episodes
of triumphs flash across the screen of past times:
There's that unkept promise that was made to me –
I'd be given a job at home when I received my degree.

Why? I never quite understood. I guess my character
wasn't too good! The principal never responded to my
application to give me that bit of information. I made
up my mind within myself. "I'll become the best damn
teacher someplace else. Yes, I Can!"

The supervisor said fourth graders couldn't do it.
Our science fair project was too broad. But one thing
she didn't realize, telling me it couldn't be done made
me more determined. So we easily won first prize.

"You can't get rid of it", I shouted. "Yes, I can! I can
create my own kind of therapy, to set my mind free".

My inner soul cried out – "How much more can you take?"
When faced with the terminal illness of my loved one.
All his previous illnesses flashed before me and I
began to scream, "Enough's enough already. I can't
handle it. No Way!" Then very faintly I heard
myself say "Yes, I Can!.

Common reasoning told me it was too late in my senior
years. No one at sixty-eight could begin a whole new
life. But the silent voice inside yelled out in pride
"Yes, I can!"

Life is never a bed of roses. Surely has not been for
me. The thorns – mixed in – add a challenge. The
greater the challenge, the sweeter the victory!

so this is my solemn creed. I'm grateful to the lowly
ant, for inspiring me to succeed when others say I can't.
"Yes, I can! I can make tomorrow better!
I can make my world better!"

# HEALING
# THOUGHTS

# FAMILY

# Family

A family is as precious as can be.
Each member is like a branch on a tree
Extending from one central point
And connecting every crucial joint . . .

To make all members become one;
Fathers, mothers, daughters and sons,
Producing offspring as budding flowers
Adding love and joy to every hour.

The times spent together can't be beat
As you laugh, have fun, joke, and eat.
Then when you part you keep in touch.
The closeness and concern mean so much.

Whenever tragedy or misfortune strikes one
The others rally to see what can be done.
You gather a lot of strength from each other.
It is so good to have sisters and brothers.

## Ode to Fluffy

You came to us on a cold wintry day.
A fuzzy little ball full of frolic and play.
Little did we know the love and joy you'd bring;
You wrapped your little paws around our heartstring.

You became our little princess and had the best,
And sometimes put our patience to the test,
When you scratched the furniture and left cat hair
On the chairs, the bed and everywhere!

You loved to sit on your "daddy's" lap,
And snuggle closely and take a nap.
He never disturbed you for one minute,
Unless there was nothing he could do to prevent it.

You brought us so much love and joy for seventeen years;
When we lost you we shed many tears,
But your presence is with us although you are gone,
And our love for you lingers on and on.

## Tribute to Roy

Not a day goes by when I don't think of you, dear.
Somehow I know your spirit is always near.
Many cherished memories flood my mind,
And that brings me calm and peace, I find.

Although your physical presence is gone,
The feelings of our togetherness linger on.
The laughter, the joys, the struggles, the tears,
All that we went through for thirty-two years.

Yes, there were bad times, but the good times were best
For our strong love always stood the test
Of the outside forces tossing us about.
With God's help things always worked out.

You taught me a lot although I didn't always agree,
But now what I learned from you is paying off for me.
To have faith in God no matter what people say,
Because He is always with us and will open the way

To the goals and success that our hearts desire,
And fill our souls with power and fire.
We should believe in His promises and keep His commands
For He's our only true friend and always understands.

I know you'll never be far from me,
You're in the surroundings and everything I see.
Your voice is hushed but the chatter lingers on,
In my memory, although you are gone.

So rest in contented peace, my love.
I sing praises for our years to the good Lord above.
One day we'll meet again, you and me,
And can praise Him together throughout eternity!

# Tribute to My Family

Those were the darkest moments of my life.
I had gone through many dark hours of strife.
But you came to my rescue with comfort and love,
Bringing peace to my heart like a mourning dove.

So many of you came to share my grief
It was heart warming and brought tremendous relief.
Nephews, nieces, in-laws, my children, sisters and
    brother,
There was a deeper bond between one another.

For such an occasion that is normally sad,
You brought joy and laughter that made me glad
To be part of a family that is as wonderful as you.
I shall always remember it my whole life through.

Your love and concern continue each day
When some of you call me just to say,
"How are you doing? We love you so.
If you ever need us, just let us know!"

God saw fit to take Roy home,
But I know I will never be alone.
With God and a family like you by my side,
I can face the future with courage and pride.

## A Wonderful Son

I remember the day you were born
On that cold bleak December morn.
When I looked into your little face
The love I felt, nothing could replace.

You were a cute, plump little bouncing boy
That brought all of us so much joy.
It only took me just a short while
To realize you were a very special child.

You proved all that as the years went by.
There was nothing you were afraid to try.
Your many unusual talents almost seem unreal;
I always wonder what your next move will reveal.

That intricate mind of yours is always in motion;
Moving on to new adventures whenever you have the
     notion.
Your dedication as a doctor to all humankind
Is your primary goal that brings you peace of mind.

There is so much pride deep down in my heart.
All the joy I feel you play the major part.
Perhaps in the past I have failed to always show it,
But somehow deep down within I think you know it.

The grandchildren you gave that fill my heart with joy
Are all a part of that little baby boy
That God blessed me with so many years ago.
Life would be empty without you because I love you so.

As I reflect on this Mother's Day,
I am so proud of you in every possible way.
And think of all the many things you have done;
I thank God for such a wonderful son.


## To Kendra on Your Special Day

How proud I was when I took the first peep
At such a lovely little girl;
With sparkling eyes and dimpled cheeks;
The most beautiful granddaughter in the world.

I knew you were a chip off the old block.
You seemed to have a way of your own.
But you came from a pretty good stock;
Now I can't believe you are full grown.

Upon this day of your graduation,
Making a major milestone in your life.
I'm proud and extend my congratulations,
And my support if you're ever faced with strife.

You are intelligent, gifted, and bright,
And you really deserve the best.
I know you'll work hard with all your might
To attain nothing but success.

You are a very special granddaughter
With a winning smile like no other.
Always hang on to that cheerful laughter.
I'm so proud to be your grandmother!

## To My Grandson Jared

I didn't forget about you, "Hon,"
Because you are a fine grandson.
I love you more than you'll ever know,
So accept this little piece of "dough."

For all the good work you've done
Throughout the year, having lots of fun.
Spend it for something nice.
Don't be a miser all your life!

And when time for your graduation comes,
You will receive a larger sum,
Just like I gave your lovely sister,
So hang in there and do good, "Mister"!

## My Daddy

My daddy was the best dad in the world.
I knew from the beginning he loved his little girl.
I remembered how I used to sit upon his knee
While he bounced me up and down so happy and free.

There were eight of us, I'm pleased to say,
And he loved each one in a very special way.
He was kind, patient, and extremely understanding
Firm in giving guidance but never demanding.

He had so much love in his big kind heart;
When it came to winning you over he was very smart.
He always had time to listen to what you had to say,
Believed in hard work, but gave us time to play.

I really loved his soft-spoken voice,
He never scolded but always gave us a choice.
His forgiving spirit was another one of his traits,
Whenever we made mistakes, he gave us time to get things
    straight.

I never heard him say "I told you so,"
Once he forgave, he'd readily let it go.
No matter what happened he was always there for me,
Giving all his help and support so willingly.

I remember him telling us how he learned to read.
His Sunday school teacher helped him fill that need.
He learned to build and skillfully use his hands,
Having no formal education, he was still a talented man.

He wanted each of us to have an education,
And was the only one to attend my college graduation.
That was one of the happiest days in my life;
My daddy had stood by me through all my strife.

I told him then he was the best daddy in the world.
He hugged my neck and told me I was his lovely girl.
All of his children brought him a lot of pride,
No matter what happened he was always by our side.

Daddy lost his sight in his later years;
I admired his courage as he seemed to have no fears.
He kept it a secret while he practiced finding his way
To every place throughout the house day by day.

All the grandchildren were his pride and joy,
He showed love and compassion to each girl and boy.
Guiding, advising, and proud of their success . . .
Wishing, hoping and praying for their happiness.

He was brave and courageous right up to the end.
We not only lost a dad, but also our best friend.
He left all of us a legacy that we can live by:
To believe in ourselves, and we can make it if we try.

I miss that loving man as each day goes by.
Sometimes so much I really want to cry,
But then I realize God knew best
And Daddy is there with Him taking his rest.

So I thank God for giving me the best dad in the world,
And one day I know that his little girl
Will be so happy to see his smiling face.
And we can love again in that beautiful place!

## I Remember Mama

When I hurt and the pain won't go away . . .
    I remember Mama
How she could touch the place and it would be gone to stay!
    Oh, how I miss Mama.

When the nightmares come and there's no one to wake
    me . . .
    I remember Mama
How she would always come in to shake me
    I miss my Mama.

When I have a problem and don't know what to do . . .
    I remember Mama
How she was always there to see me through . . .
    I surely need Mama.

I remember the time she wished she could take my place
    Oh, what a caring Mama!
When another operation I had to face . . .
    She was a loving Mama.

Sometimes she chided a lot and I didn't understand . . .
    But now I do Mama.
She only wanted the best for her entire clan.
    Thank you so much, Mama.

She reared all of us then started with the "grands"
    How did you do it, Mama?
She seemed to have it all included in her plans . . .
    Such a caring Mama.

I can't forget how it made her so glad . . .
    I remember it all, Mama.
When I'd go home and the long talks we had . . .
    I miss those talks, Mama.

Sometimes I pretend that she is here . . .
    And I talk to Mama.
I imagine I hear her voice so dear . . .
    I love you Mama.


## A Loving Sister

All my sisters are very caring
But there is one that's special to me.
She always knows when I need her most.
Just talking with her makes my troubles flee.

We seem to have a special bond.
That tells us when the other is in trouble.
She never fails to say she loves me,
And for her that goes double.

So when I'm really feeling down,
And my burdens are so hard to bear.
She always comes through for me,
All my burdens, she is willing to share.

I am grateful for such a loving sister
And pray that our love will never wane.
I don't know what I'd do without her.
My life really wouldn't be the same.

# Danny Boy

He was special to me and brought so much joy.
Even when he was just a tiny boy.
We had a little kissing game we always played.
I can't forget the impact on my life he's made.

Years passed by and the love for each other grew.
Deep down within, somehow I always knew,
That a special place in my heart he'd won.
He was not just a nephew, but more like a son!

He was concerned about me and did things on my behalf.
No matter how sad I felt he could always make me laugh.
He was filled with love, compassion and joy.
Yes, he was my nephew, my little Danny Boy.

My Danny Boy had an attentive ear
Whenever I was burdened with fear.
His words of comfort were always just right,
And helped to make my burdens light.

He was there for me during a bad time in my life
When I was going through a lot of pain and strife.
Finally the pain was over and it made his heart glad.
I knew he was the best nephew I ever had.

My Danny Boy still makes me rejoice
When I pick up the phone and hear his voice.
We laugh and giggle and talk about the past.
I knew the love that started then will always last!

# My Three Guys

My three handsome guys
Are cunning and wise.
They always keep me company
Without ever crowding me.

There never is a lot of chatter,
And that really doesn't matter.
Their quiet presence is all I need,
They are a very special breed.

Their eyes are dark and caring,
Showing me they are sharing
My feelings of loneliness, sadness, and joy.
I don't know what I'd do without my boys.

I hug their little cuddly bodies each night,
And just before I turn out the light
I bow and say a prayer religiously,
"Lord, watch over Sam, Bubba, Danny, and me."

Each morning when I hear the clock alarm,
I know God has kept us from all harm,
Because their faces are the first thing I see,
There by my side, smiling back at me.

Although they are just three teddy bears
Deep in my heart I know each one cares
As real beings, not just a toy,
Because they bring such comfort and joy.

# EARLY
# CHILDHOOD
# MEMORIES

# The Old Farm

Memories of that little old farm
Still haunt me through the years.
The hills, woods, and house with its charm,
Sometimes so vivid my eyes fill with tears.

The lovely farm was the place of my birth,
Where good times were experienced by all.
It was the most beautiful place on earth
In winter, spring, summer, and fall.

In the old farmhouse sitting on the hill,
Busy activities, laughter and love were found.
All that we did brought such a thrill;
Even the farm animals made happy sounds.

Whinnying in the barnyard was the old horse Kate,
Bossy, the cow, in the pasture mooing;
A cat meowing, looking for its mate,
A block of pigeons on the rooftop cooing.

Frogs were croaking and crickets were singing
Butterflies and bees tasted the flowers.
The branches on the trees were neatly clinging
As the old crow bounced on them for hours.

Sitting with a fishing pole by the riverbank
While the birds chirped in the nearby woods.
A fish nibbled and the stopper sank,
Boy, I knew I had caught him for good!

A winding road lined with cedar trees
Led out to a lonely highway.
The trees were beautiful as they bowed in the breeze
On hot days we'd sit under them and play.

So often I go on those minute vacations
Back to that lovely old farm.
It was just like a storybook plantation,
With all the adventure, mystery, and charm.

## Childhood Fantasy Come True

When I was just a little girl
I'd lose myself in a fantasy world.
I pretended I was teaching school,
All the lessons and enforcing each rule.

I made my classroom enclosed with rocks.
My students were sticks on little blocks.
For hours I would instruct and teach,
Earnestly giving special help to each.

I proudly hung on to this fantasy
And finally my dream became a reality.
I became a teacher with real kids to teach.
Through many trials, my goal, I was determined to reach.

When the day came and I stood before my class,
I breathed a prayer of thanks, I was there at last,
There sat thirty real kids with smiling faces,
In thirty real seats all in their places.

So my advice to anyone who has a childhood dream,
Hold on to it for dear life no matter how hard it seems.
Work hard, persevere, and it will happen to you,
Your childhood fantasy surely can come true.

## The Little Country Church

I remember the little church of long ago,
Nestled among a cluster of trees.
I learned things about God that I didn't know,
And it was Him I wanted to please.

In that little building made of wood
Where a narrow dusty road went by;
The services and fellowship were good
And lifted our spirits high.

The old-fashioned revivals were the best
And were held during the summertime
I wanted to be able to stand God's test,
So I knelt with others in the saving line.

They sang "Amazing Grace How Sweet the Sound."
I wanted God to save a wretch like me.
I was lost and desired to be found;
Was blind and anxious to see!

God reached out that night and saved my soul;
Blessed me with His amazing grace.
Since then I've been running to reach my goal.
So one day I'll see Him face to face.

## The Old Oak Tree

The old oak tree stood proud and tall,
With its sturdy branches reaching out
Like arms extending forth to call
All creatures wandering about.

It was home for the old hoot owl,
The robin, cardinal, and blue jay.
And many other beautiful fowl
That stopped for a rest on their way.

It had withstood many storms in the past,
Bending its head when the strong winds came;
Then raised its branches high to cast
Shade for a lot of wild game.

On one of its branches was a child's homemade swing
That had provided many hours of fun.
God created that old oak tree so it could bring
Protection, joy, and comfort to everyone.

# The Little Schoolhouse

The little, old three-room school
Beside a lonely, winding dirt road,
Was where I received my very first rules
In learning to carry life's load.

I leard the three R's and my ABCs,
But socially I was very shy.
However, I worked extremely hard to please,
And did my best to try.

I was obedient and did my work well.
Was brave enough to join the cheering squad.
Learned my math and how to read and spell,
And behaved myself on the school yard.

I sang well enough to be in the glee club;
And learned to develop my voice.
Hated the outside toilets we had to scrub,
Because we were assigned, and had no choice.

We had a good time playing games.
I learned a lot from the older girls.
Things they told me were always the same
About what I'd have to face in this world.

The foundation was laid for what I became
In that little old three-room school.
And brought much happiness, if not a lot of fame.
I'm so glad I followed all the rules.

# CONVERSATIONS WITH GOD

## Alone with God

In the quiet stillness of the early morn
Visions of new goals and insights are born.
My strength for the day is fortified
With God patiently sitting by my side.

Not a single sound can be heard;
Just me and God and His holy word;
As I read my Bible and meditate,
Realizing nothing else could duplicate . . .

This quiet time and fruitful thoughts,
Something so precious cannot be bought.
Feelings of fear and anxiety disappear,
Because I know my God is near.

I look forward to my time alone with God,
Preparing myself for the road I must trod.
I know He will guide me along the way,
So I meet with Him before I begin my day.

# Speak to Me, God

Speak to me, God
   When my heart is heavy with grief,
   And I can't seem to find relief.
   I've cried until tears won't come
   Over the loss of my loved one.

Speak to me, God
   Tell me the hurt will go away,
   And there will be a better day.
   Tell me that You feel my pain,
   That I will be able to laugh again.

Speak to me, God
   Speak to my broken heart.
   Tell me I can make a new start.
   That the loneliness will subside,
   And with me, You will abide.

Speak to me, God
   Give me Your strong hand to hold,
   And let Your love flood my soul,
   With the assurance, my heart You'll mend.
   And You will always be my friend.

Speak to me, God
   Give me Your forgiveness for feeling doubt.
   I know You will always help me out.
   It's just that I'm weak in my sorrow,
   And have all these fears about tomorrow.

Speak to me, God
   Say You understand just how I feel.
   Tell me my broken heart will heal.
   And I will be able to happily live.
   Because of all the love You give.

## Thank You Lord

Thank You dear Lord
For making me so glad.
You helped me discover a talent
That I didn't know I had.

When I asked You in sincere prayer
For something to fill the lonely hours
I only expected a sprinkle of blessings
And You lovingly gave me showers.

Now, O Lord, please help me use
My talents to Your will and pleasure.
May I always show my gratitude
For something I will always treasure.


## Walk with Me, Lord

Lord, I need You to walk before me
To prepare the rugged way,
Or else I won't be able
To get through every day.

I need You to walk beside me
So I'll have someone to lean on
To make sure I don't stumble and fall
As I travel the whole day long.

And Lord, walk behind me
To clean up all my mistakes.
I just need You all around me
Do this for Jesus' sake!

# A Morning Prayer

Lord, I wake to face a new day
Help me through each minute, I pray.
Guide my actions and my speech,
Wherever I can, let me teach . . .

Someone about Your blessings of love
That You shower on us from above.
Telling others that I meet
About all the promises that You keep.

How You love us and always care,
And our burdens You gladly share.
That no problems we'll have to face,
Without Your tender mercy and saving grace.

Then, dear Lord, when day is done
At the setting of the sun,
When the day fades into night,
Your love will be our shining light.

This we know from times gone by
We are always under Your watchful eye.
You'll watch over us as we sleep,
And our souls You'll tenderly keep.

Amen

# Enough for Me

Some are not sure about their souls,
They wonder if any good their hearts can hold.
But I know Christ died upon a tree,
And gave His life to set us free,
    And that's enough for me!

Some are not sure about a heavenly home,
And fail to realize they are never alone.
But I know Christ promised to always be
Right by my side to fill my heart with glee,
    And that's enough for me!

Some overlook the fact Christ never lies.
They don't believe He hears each one that cries.
But I know He hears my humble plea,
And will constantly make my burdens flee.
    And that's enough for me!

Some wander through an entire lifetime,
Finding it hard to make up their minds.
They are never sure about their spirituality,
But with Christ in my heart I can plainly see.
    And that's enough for me!

# The Invisible Passenger

Each time that I decide
To take a trip in my car,
Whether it is near
Or whether it is far,

I always take the time
To buckle myself in;
Then I look in the vacant seat,
And there sits my friend.

Although I cannot see Him
I know that He is there,
To guide and protect me,
And to relieve every care.

He is with me when I'm traveling
Over the long dangerous highway,
So everytime before cranking my car
I always take time to pray . . .

"Dear Lord, please ride with me
And protect me from all harm.
Help me drive with care and caution
Without facing fear or alarm."

When I reach my destination
I never get out of my car
Before bowing my head to thank Him
For being my guiding star.

## Why Me, Lord?

Why me, Lord, I continue to ask
Why am I given this impossible task?
I am weak in my body and spirit as well.
How I will make it, I cannot tell.

How, Lord? How can I get the job done?
I look for help and there is none.
So I pause right now in sincere prayer
To ask if You really care . . .

About the heavy load I'm carrying
And the rugged path I'm tarrying.
Hear me Lord! Hear my cry . . .
Let me know You are standing by.

Thank You, Lord, I can hear You speak.
My faith in You became a little weak.
You promised to help, and You do not lie;
So I had no need to ask You why!

Because You promised in Your holy word
That every prayer would be heard.
And You would come to help us out;
There was no need for me to doubt.

# A Walk with God

The warm spring breeze was kissing my face.
The sweet smell of lilac whiffed past my nose.
I walked more swiftly, increasing my pace,
Touching the velvety petals of each rose.

An array of colors blended together,
A sure sign of the approaching spring weather.
Row after row, each flower seemed to bow.
I whispered, "I'm walking with God right now."

He was speaking to me through the flowers.
I became so engrossed I walked with Him for hours,
I stopped to marvel at the beauty of some clover,
And felt so relaxed when our walk was over.

Now when I am tense, I must confess
I walk among my flowers to ease the stress.
I have the assurance that God meets me there,
Communes with me and relieves despair.

## My Guardian Angel

There are many times I have no doubt
When things happen that I cannot explain,
I have a Guardian Angel who helps me out,
And gets me on the right track again.

Sometimes I feel His guiding hand
Leading me in the right direction.
Although I don't quite understand
How He makes all the corrections . . .

Of all the mistakes that I have made;
Sometimes, seemingly beyond repair.
But somehow all the dark shadows fade,
Because my Guardian Angel is there.

## God Is My Strength

When I find myself becoming bogged down
In a marshland of despair;
Too weak for answers to be found,
I turn to God in prayer.

God is my strength in times like these.
I know He will always be there.
So I simply stop and fall on my knees,
And ask for His help in prayer.

He's my strength, my help, my guide
When I am carrying a heavy load.
He is always there by my side
As I travel life's rocky road.

## My Plea

Lord, help me to live all my days
By showing your love in many ways.
Give me courage to smile when I should frown
Let me lift one's spirit when they're feeling down.

Let my faith shine through when things are tough.
Help me to realize when I've had enough;
Then I will know how much I need your help
And remember all the promises you have kept.

Lord, in my feeble efforts should I fail
And You have tried to help me to no avail.
Please forgive and stand by me . . .
And try me one more time . . . is my plea.

## Just for You, Lord

Just for You, Lord, my heart beats,
Prayerfully hoping I'll be able to meet
My obligations in doing the task
Of all the things that You ask

Just for You, Lord, my heart pleads
For my fellowman to take heed
To follow Your will and obey Your command,
And fit their lives into Your plan.

Just for You, Lord, my heart swells
When You assure me that all is well;
That I will have nothing to fear,
Because You will always be near.

Just for You, Lord, my heart pines
For Your love and mercy all the time.
That I will always have strength to do
All the things You expect me to.

Just for You, Lord, my heart rejoices
That You always hear Your children's voices
Whenever we call upon Your name,
Your response of mercy is always the same.

## At the Crossroad

I'm standing here at life's crossroad,
And I'm burdened with a heavy load.
There are so many decisions I must make,
I do not know what steps to take.

It's a lonely and distressing predicament to be in;
Standing here not knowing where to begin.
"I really need your help, Lord," I pray.
"Only You can help me find my way."

Then I hear His soft sweet voice,
Saying, "My child, I'll help you make a choice.
All you have to do is free your mind,
And learn to take one day at a time."

So I take heed to my Master's voice,
And realize now I don't have to make a choice.
For whenever I do have to decide,
My Master will be there as my guide.

My fears are gone now, I don't worry,
I know nothing has to be done in a hurry.
My Master will see me through all my strife,
As I stand here at the crossroad of my life.

# A Little Talk with God

When troubles overshadow my vision
I quickly come to the decision
    I need a little talk with God.

If I am filled with despair,
I turn to someone who really cares
    So I have a little talk with God.

When I'm burdened with a heavy load
Traveling over a rough rocky road,
    I pause to have a little talk with God.

When my body is racked with pain,
And the doctors cannot explain,
    All I need is a talk with God.

Of all life's fears I have to face,
Nothing else can take the place
    Of my little talks with God.

When I'm faced with a mountain to climb
And some help I need to find,
    I ask in my little talk with God.

## The Lord Is My Shepherd

The Lord is my Shepherd
He never lets me want too long.
He leads me through green gardens,
And fills my heart with song.

The waters are still and peaceful,
Where he gently restores my soul.
The paths of righteousness where He leads me
Are paved with blessings untold.

When walking through the dark valley
No evil will I ever fear.
His rod and staff will comfort me;
I'm assured he will always be near.

Although my enemies are present,
He prepares a table that we may sup.
And anoints my head with sweet smelling oil,
And over runs my cup.

Because the Lord is my Shepherd,
Goodness and mercy will follow me.
I will be blessed all the days of my life,
And I will dwell in His house throughout eternity.

# Bridle My Tongue, Lord

Bridle my tongue, Lord
When an argument becomes heated.
Help me stay composed and calm,
And not feel that I am defeated.

Bridle my tongue, Lord
When others are scandalizing one's name.
Let me speak good about others,
Because I could be treated the same.

Bridle my tongue, Lord
When I am falsely accused.
As long as You know the truth about me.
You will not let my name be abused.

Bridle my tongue, Lord
When I am in the presence of sin.
Please help me to keep silent,
And refrain from joining in.

Use my tongue, Lord
To always speak words of praise,
Remembering good deeds can come back to me,
And bless me for the rest of my days.

## Using My Senses

Let me use my eyes to see
Not only the beauty of nature around me,
But also the destruction and blight,
And everything that isn't right.

That I might do whatever I can
To make life better for my fellowman,
By giving a helping hand to someone in need,
Regardless of race, color or creed.

Let me use my ears to hear
The cry of those who are filled with fear.
May I speak words of comfort and peace
And all fears and heartaches will cease.

Let me hear the sweet songs of birds,
And my Master's comforting words.
To bring peace and joy to my heart,
Causing all negative thoughts to depart.

Let me use my nose to smell
The sweet aroma of flowers that I love so well.
May I use it to warn me of dangers that are near
To help protect me from things I fear.

May I keep my nose out of the business of others;
And treat them all like sisters and brothers.
Instead of constantly sniffing around
To see what hidden dirt can be found.

Let me use my mouth to taste
God's nourishing food without haste
In gobbling it down and asking for more,
Never concerned about the hungry and poor.

Let me never use my mouth to speak
Words of discouragement to those who are weak.
May words of my mouth and meditation of my heart
Help someone to make a good start.

Let my hands reach out and touch
Someone who needs my love so much.
May I be able to feel their pain and sorrow.
And help them strive for a better tomorrow.

May I use my hands to do good deeds,
Helping others to secure their needs;
To be an extension of God's strong hands
Working faithfully to carry out His plans.

# FEELINGS

# Tranquility

I never thought a tree could be
An object of such tranquility.
My eyes steadily feasting
Upon the tall sturdy pine tree
Calmly soaked in the serene beauty,
As I watched the sunbeams
Bathe the clumps of snow
That were artistically clinging
On to the green branches all aglow.

A peace and calmness flooded over me
Bringing about a feeling of such tranquility
Of being so close to God . . .
Being touched by Him.
A tranquil peace that only He
Could bring through nature.

Watching the snowcapped branches
Swaying as a gentle breeze
Flowed through them
Gave me a floating sensation. . . .
My mind drifted into a panorama
Of the stages of the old pine tree
Beginning with a tiny seed. . . .

That had been nourished by God . . .
Bursting forth to grow stage by stage
In such an orderly way
Sharing its beauty day by day
Only God could make that tree
To bring such tranquility!

# Grief Has a Logic of Its Own

Grief. . . . nobody wants to
    experience or face it.
But it comes . . . and it's real.
Something is needed to help it heal.
You must find something to replace it.

Grief has a logic of its own.
    It always seems to come too soon. . . .
    Catching you off guard . . .
    Hitting hard . . . on your emotions.

How do you deal with it?
    Put it aside . . . pretend it's not there?
    It will only smolder inside . . .
    Causing more despair.

Will you put up a front of being strong? . . .
    When really there's an emptiness and
    Hopelessness; everything going wrong.

The logic of grief is real . . .
You must give in to what you feel.
How will you do it? . . . no one can say.
Each may do it a different way.
Some cry, get angry, break things, curse, or pray.

Others may feel that they can dodge it
By getting involved in some new project.

No one sure method is cut and dried,
But you can rest assured God will be by your side.
The right way for each to handle it is unknown,
Because grief has a logic of its own.

## Sorrow

Sorrow is an emotion we don't like to face.
We would rather that it passed us by,
But we know as we run this life's race
We must face it no matter how hard we try.

Life must have its portion of sorrow.
That's the way God intended it to be.
It's here today but will be gone tomorrow
And again our hearts can be free.

The sorrows of life help us to appreciate
All the joy that comes in its place.
As we calmly and gratefully meditate
On God's unchanging grace.

We must carry our sorrows lightly
And remember Christ had his sorrows, too.
But the light of hope will shine brightly,
And help us to see it through.

## Silence

There is power and beauty in silence;
It is all about being quiet, still, serene . . .
To hear God's still small voice
That will give guidance
And power to achieve
And in His holy word believe.

Enabling us to hear sounds of beauty
And to see a beauty
Transcending outer appearances
Of nature and people around us . . .
Enhancing the power to relate
To all of God's creation.

Silence . . . the quiet time to meditate
And commune with God . . .
Helps to receive a roadmap for life
Giving us the power to read
And follow in reaching our dreams.

We pause along the way
To usurp the beauty of life each day
Giving us the power to get beyond self
Fitting into God's plans for us
To grow in strength and knowledge
According to His will
Always taking time to be still
Keeping ever before us
There is power and beauty in silence!

## Remembering a Loved One

Thanks for memories so precious and dear
They are still with me although you are not here.
The times when we laughed with our hearts full of cheer,
How we weathered life's storms that were always lurking
    near.

Together we worked and strived to succeed
In all our undertakings to supply all our needs.
There were times when we smiled and times when we
    cried,
But we always made it through with God by our side.

## Feelings

All day long my feelings go,
Back and forth, to and fro.
Sadness, frustration, pain, and sorrow,
Wondering what fate lies in store for tomorrow.

Then suddenly joy creeps through my mind,
Leaving all the sad thoughts behind.
I dwell on the present and forget about the past.
No thoughts about tomorrow because no pain will last.

As long as I keep Christ the center of my thoughts,
The battles of despair can easily be fought.
No burdens will be too heavy to bear or face,
Because of His tender mercy and loving grace.

So I let go of my feelings of mixed emotions,
And bow on my knees in humble devotion,
To thank the Almighty who is always near,
To calm my heart when it's filled with fear.

# An Attack of Depression

Loneliness—feeling that I belong nowhere
Filled with uncertain fear,
Of now, the future—forever!

Afraid to go on . . .
Something pulling me in all directions
Needing a shield for protection
From hurt and rejection.
Afraid to look forward,
Daring to look back;
Frozen in my tracks.

Self-pity and hopelessness
Swooping over me like a dark cloud,
Wishing there was something to make me proud
To be alive . . . and thrive
In the sunshine of success,
But my life is a mess!

Depression is consuming me.
I long to be free.
I need hope
To help me cope
With the sudden mixed feelings
That send me reeling
Into despondency!

And then I say
There is a way.
So I turn my thoughts within
And find a loving friend
Who will relieve all despair,
Because He cares.

He knows all about my inner feelings
Of sorrow, hurt, and pain
And will help me regain
A new zest for life, and living
To do His will.

Yes, God is the answer
To ease the stress
When I am depressed.
He is able
To make me stable,
Courageous and strong
To face life head-on!

## Searching for Myself

Who am I?
What am I about?
Just a little speck in this vast universe?
Where do I fit in?

I search deep down in my soul
To explore my inner self,
Looking for something on which to hold,
To bring forth the real me . . .
And then I see . . .

I am God's creation
There is only one like me . . . I'm special.
I'm about love . . . feelings . . . emotions . . . desires.
Love for God, my fellowman, for myself
Boils inside of me
Ready to erupt and be free,
To land where it serves best.

Multiple feelings hidden in my big kind heart,
Eager and anxious to do their part
To make me special to someone who needs me.
All these beautiful things I see.

I am no longer a little speck
In this vast universe.
I have emotions . . . I can feel hurt and pain,
Even fear, hate and worry may creep in,
But I have the ability to regain
A peaceful coexistence with feelings
Of joy, contentment, peace and happiness.

In my search I find desires
Hidden away waiting to burst forth
And light the fires
Of passion and romance
If given a chance.

And where do I fit in?
Anywhere, anyplace, yet some special place
Where God needs me
To do a special job
That can only be done by me.

Inside of me is simple, yet complicated,
With vast potentials for . . .
Loving, caring, sharing, giving and forgiving
I am deep, yet shallow
Because these feelings
Are easily aroused.
Amazing . . . how so much can be housed
In the pint-sized person that I am.

# A Look into Your Heart

The little organ
Inside your chest,
Often taken for granted,
But it is the best,
It sustains life—the very center of your being.

It is small, yet big—holding so much.
Without it you are out of touch
With what you are
Or what you can be.
A look into your heart reveals an eternity . . .
A beginning and an ending and a forever!

The little organ—your heart . . .
Is a palace
Holding your morality . . . your spirituality . . .
Your mortality and immortality!

There inside lie seeds of human attributes
That constitute
Your very soul.
Love, kindness, forgiveness and others
Waiting for you to nourish,
That they may blossom into
What God, the Creator, expects of you.

A look into your heart
Will reveal emotions
That enhance deep devotion
For God and your fellowman
That will a lifetime span
And even into the promised land.

Seeing all this in your heart
You dare not start
Allowing the deadly seeds
To be planted that will produce weeds
Of hate, prejudice, malice, and greed;
Allowing sin to creep in.

Your heart is precious to hold . . .
It is the essence of your soul!


## My Security Blanket

I am grateful to God for a wonderful gift
That I can always use to give me a lift.
It's a security blanket I can hold on to
For boosting my morale when I feel sad and blue.

Whenever major problems fill me with fear.
I write poetry about it and it will disappear.
Words just seem to flow bringing answers to my mind;
Soon all my problems are left behind.

Writing poetry not only helps when I'm feeling sad,
It's also a way of expressing myself when I'm glad.
When nobody is around to tell about the joy I feel,
I can write it down and it is just as real.

My faithful companions are my paper and pen.
I communicate with them for hours on end.
And when I finish I feel happy and complete.
A feeling of fulfillment over my whole being sweeps.

So my security blanket warms my heart when it's cold.
Whenever I'm frightened it helps put my fears on hold.
I am grateful to God for giving me this gift,
Because it never fails to give me a lift!

## Life's Uncertainties

Life is uncertain with its twists and turns.
One knows not how things will turn out.
We must be willing to wait and learn
To trust in God and ease our doubts.

It's not in His will for us to see the end,
When faced with the tumultuous storms of life.
Faith and courage will help you to begin
To strive to deal with all fears and strife.

There will be a lot of pitfalls along the way,
But nothing can stop you from going on.
Your darkness will soon be turned into day,
Because it's always darkest before the dawn.

So keep your wits intact no matter how hard it seems.
And work faithfully with all your might.
That is a sure way to realize all your dreams,
And everything will turn out all right.

# The School of Hard Knocks

I have a degree from the school of hard knocks,
And I am very proud to say
I got over all the stumbling blocks
Because I learned how to pray.

I passed the courses in endurance
No matter how hard the task,
Because my Savior gave me the assurance
That the hard times would not last.

I made good grades in perseverance
Success was my ultimate goal.
Failure took on a different appearance
As my future began to unfold.

My degree from the school of hard knocks
Is hanging on the walls of my heart.
I praise God for getting me over stumbling blocks
Because He played the major part.

## Today

Today has twenty-four hours in it,
Cram all you can into every minute.
Ounces of smiles with everyone you meet,
As you walk along the street.

Pounds of patience with your fellowman;
Giving all the love you can.
Adding pints of sharing, too;
What you give will come back to you.

Quarts of understanding will be just fine,
Bringing many of your friends peace of mind.
A gallon of forgiveness for unkind deeds;
Doing God's will, to His words take heed.

Pecks of kindness, throw all around,
Many who need it can be found.
A bushel of thoughtfulness will make someone glad,
Whenever they may be feeling sad.

Just think of how each little measure
Can fill your day with lots of pleasure,
So use them daily in all your dealings
You'll find the results can be quite appealing.

## Mirror of the Soul

The eyes show our true emotions
Reflecting every little hidden feeling
Of love, caring, and ardent devotion,
Or some that are not quite so appealing.

The eyes are the mirror of the soul
They may show fear, excitement, and gladness;
Even signs of growing old,
Anger, deceit, guilt, and sadness.

So when I look into your eyes
I see your true feelings unfold,
Overshadowing disguises, cover-ups or lies,
Because the eyes are the mirror of your soul.


## Look Back, but No Regrets

There is no harm to look back at times.
It really helps us to clear our minds.
But we must never have regrets
About the things we should forget.

The past is gone so let it stay there.
Dealing with the present is enough to bear.
So don't ever linger on the past too long
Or you will find your present going wrong.

If we could change the past it would be great,
But that is impossible, it is too late.
And if by chance your past doesn't suit you,
Strive in the present for a better future.

## No Fear of Death

When the time comes
For the setting of our earthly sun
Let no fear invade your mind,
Don't worry about what's left behind.

There is no need for us to dread
The unknown fate that lies ahead.
We know that man was born to die
That can't be changed no matter how we try.

One consoling thought can always be,
Christ took the sting out of death for you and me.
So we think of it as an open door,
That we pass through to receive much more.

We should have no fear of the unknown
Because of the love our Lord has shown.
He promised us a home and we should believe it,
But we must pass through death's door to receive it.

# Prejudice

Prejudice is a word with an evil sound,
But everyone is prejudiced toward something, we've
    found.
Either some foods, actions or clothing we wear,
But when it's focused on people, it's hard to bear.

Why hate because of the color of one's skin,
When in God's sight we all are kin?
We are His children, He made us all,
To despise one another can be your downfall.

God made us different, we don't know why.
He had His reasons and we should try
To accept His will and live as sisters and brothers;
And show respect, love, and kindness to each other.

Some hate others because of their religion or creed.
But what does it matter, there is no need,
Because each has a right to a faith of his own.
Everyone is striving to reach the same heavenly home.

So what are you going to do when we all get there?
Do you really think God is going to care . . .
Whether you're Baptist or Catholic, white, black, or brown?
He will be there to give all of us a crown!

So why not put all your prejudice aside;
And let us live together with dignity and pride . . .
As God's children carrying out His command
That we might live better in that promised land.

# Guilt

Guilt is like a cancer
Eating away at your heart and mind.
Bringing a lot of misery and pain;
A cure, you need to find.

You can bring an end to it all
And find a way to erase it
Let go and let God take over
And let forgiveness replace it.

Once you have cleared your mind
And have forgiven yourself;
Then you can move forward
To forgive everybody else.

There is no need to look back
And feel guilty about the past,
When you forgive yourself,
You'll have a cure that will last.

# Meditation

Sitting quietly, closing my eyes,
Blotting out visions of the outside world,
Erasing all disturbing thoughts from my mind
Drifting slowly into deep meditation . . . .

I let every muscle in my body relax
Easing deeper and deeper into my inner self
I am totally free now . . .
Free and uninhibited. . . .

Free as a wild stallion
Galloping across the open plains, nostrils flared . . .
Shiny tail and mane, soaking up the sunlight . . .
Flowing in the wind. . . .

Muscles rippling as it glides gracefully . . .
Hoofs beating a staccato rhythm
That can be heard miles away . . .
Leaving a cloud of dust trailing behind. . . .

In the same way my mind
Is leaving the cares of life behind.
I move swiftly beyond myself
And now in tune with God, my creator . . .

Who reveals who I am and what I can become
It is so beautiful and peaceful
An aura of radiant light
And contentment surrounds me.

A new surge of energy wells inside me.
I'd like to stay here indefinitely.
But I feel certain I can deal with life's cares
When I return to reality!

# FRIENDSHIP

# True Friends

True friends will laugh with you when you're happy,
Cry with you when you are sad.
They will be with you at all times
Whether things are good or bad.

They overlook your faults and see the good
Forgive you when they're misunderstood.
Never find a need to judge,
Or ever hold on to a grudge.

They will all your secrets share.
When you need them, they'll be there.
They will always be around
To lift your spirits when you're feeling down.

They will help you bear each bitter cup,
When you fall they will help you up.
And never expect anything in return,
But always showing devotion and concern.

Winter, summer, spring, or fall,
You can depend on them to call
To kindly say, "I'm here if you need me,
No matter what the hour may be."

You are always sure you have them
Right by your side when things are dim.
They'll be with you until the bitter end,
Truly, you can call them a true friend.

# Friendship

Friendship is a two-way street.
A little bit of give and a little bit of take
From people throughout life you meet.
It helps strengthen relationships you make.

Everybody needs a friend
To tell their troubles to,
When the cares of life are closing in,
And they don't know what to do.

True friendship will stand the test
Whenever things are going wrong.
If it is one of the best,
The ties will remain strong.

Sometimes friends will let you down
Whenever you are most in need.
So the best friend that can be found
Is one of a special breed.

That best friend is Jesus,
Who is always standing by.
He will be right there to please us
When He hears our humble cry.

## Choose the Right Friends

Be careful about the friends you choose,
Or you may find you have a lot to lose,
By being friends with the class clown
Who is always fooling around.

He'll mess around and get you in trouble.
When punishment comes it will go double;
Although you have done nothing wrong.
Finding he's not a friend won't take long.

He will look you square in the face,
But will do nothing to plead your case.
Then you are left out on a limb.
Tell me, who needs a friend like him?

So be able to stand on your own two feet.
Try to evaluate the people you meet.
If their values don't satisfy,
It will be best to pass them by!

# LOVE AND
# PASSION

# Where Did Our Love Go?

It was so beautiful, solid and strong
A bond I thought could never be broken,
Our love would last forever . . . and then it happened,
So suddenly . . . our feelings . . . rushing against
The swift currents of petty things . . .
And the pull of mistrust, could no longer survive.

We were two souls drifting in opposite directions,
Like strangers passing in the night.
As I remember, the pain intensifies,
Bringing tears to my eyes. . . .
Choking out the visions of times
When we laughed together, and held each other
In moments of deep passion.
Two hearts beating as one,
Love could be heard without uttering a word.

Now there are no sparks left,
Life is no sunny day in the park.
My mind struggles to flee
From the hurt tugging at my heart.
I close my eyes, hoping sleep will make it go away.
Memories of happier times invade my dreams,
But when I awake, I have to face the reality
That our love is just a distant memory.
Where did our love go?

# The Young Lovers

They were strolling through the park . . . happy as a lark,
Hands entwined . . . one white . . . one black,
Caught up in the blissful moments,
Oblivious of the outside world staring at them.

In their late teens, their innocence was refreshing,
Heart warming, expressing a love transcending the exterior,
Penetrating the interior of each other's hearts;
Blossoming forth into loving chatter and smiling eyes
Showing the love they shared, and how much they cared.

Questions begin to erupt in my mind
About their families, perhaps full of doubt,
Wondering how this love affair will turn out.
Could their love be battered by prejudice and hate?
O dear God up above . . .
Will our cruel society assault their young love?

Are they right, and the majority wrong?
A host of questions keeps flooding my mind.
Should all love be color-blind
Like God's love for all humankind?

What a predicament we would be in
If our heavenly Father failed to love us
Because of the color of our skin.
And why are we unable to see
The Christlike love in the eyes
Of the two young lovers?

## First Love

It's a once in a lifetime experience
That first love . . . when you come face to face
With the girl or guy of your dreams
Time stands still it seems.

The rapid pounding of your heart
Is so overwhelming you lose control
As desires and passion
Sweep over your entire being.

Destiny and time
Have brought two hearts together
To merge as one soul and mind.

The first love grows and grows
In depth, width and height
Withstanding many trials
Until the outside forces
Begin tugging at it . . . distorting it.

Your lives go in opposite directions
But the feelings of that first love
Never change when you part.
You just tuck them away
In a very special place in your heart.

You may fall in love a thousand times more,
But none of them will be like before,
Or can ever take the place
Of that first love!

# The Paradoxes of Love

Love . . . all that it is . . . what it does . . .
   and represents . . . the way it makes
    us feel . . . the things it makes us do . . .
      Somewhat frightening at times!

The little four-letter word . . .
Packed with so many meanings . . .
Mixed feelings and consequences . . .
Resulting from what triggers a response
Or reaction to it . . .
      Extremely confusing at times!

There are endless paradoxes of love . . .
Bringing stress to the mind . . .
As we struggle to unscramble everything . . .
     Very frustrating at times!

There are both positive and negative feelings
   generated by love:
Love heals . . . but hurts
Brings joy . . . and sorrow, too . . .
Enhances enthusiasm, followed by hopelessness
Causes despair . . . but our hopes renew.

Smiles and laughter are results of love . . .
But then there are also tears and frowns . . .
Happiness comes . . . but soon sadness crashes dow:
It soothes and calms, yet inflames and irritates
Puts our emotions on a roller coaster . . .
And our feelings, dictate.

Love builds up and tears down . . .
Revives and drowns . . .
Brings sunshine and rain . . .
Heartaches and pain!

Causes death . . . extends life . . .
Saves and destroys . . .
Peace follows confusion . . .
Triumph overshadows tragedy . . .
All because of love!

The negative paradoxes and painful aspects related to
     love . . .
Diminish when the positive ones rise above.
We can overcome because it's true . . .
The best part of love will always burst through.
Loving . . . and being in love will survive
Because love is the foundation of our lives!


## Silhouette

Hugging my pillow tightly,
Drifting off into deep sleep,
Gliding down the path to dreamland
To a world of passion and romance.

Just dreaming . . . very soon
I glance across a dimly lit room . . .
Vaguely I see a silhouette . . .
Just a silhouette . . . but I know it's you!

Because of the rapid beating of my heart . . .
As I feel the vibrations start . . .
I begin to float forward . . . flushed . . .
But nice and tingly—this can't be rushed . . .
Must hold on to each precious minute!

I inch closer and closer . . . I'm finally there.
I can't see your face . . . just a silhouette. . . .
But then we embrace . . .
Soft music is playing . . . it's our song.
We whirl round and round across the floor,
Moving slowly through a door.

Down the stairs we stroll, hand in hand
To a quiet beach of beautiful white sand.
A crescent moon is hanging in a clear western sky . . .
Sea gulls are swooping by.

A million stars are twinkling above;
Smiling down on our strong love.
The moist breeze kisses our face
As we race along the beach . . .
Holding hands . . . falling down in the sand. . . .

Rolling over and over . . . we stop. . . .
I feel your hot kisses . . . consuming me . . .
And reach out to touch your face. . . .
But it's just a silhouette . . . it moves away
Oh, how I want it to stay!

We reach out to each other . . . struggling . . .
Trying to hold on. . . .
But then it's gone!

Suddenly I awake . . . breathless . . .
In a deep, warm sweat . . .
Remembering the silhouette.
I knew it had to be you . . .
No one else can make my heart
        pound the way you do!

## When Love Is Gone

When love dies
It's like an arrow piercing your heart. . . .
A part of you dies with it.
Life seems to come to a screeching halt.

Nothing is the same anymore
Being without love closes the door
To the happiness and joy
That was once yours.

Hopeless feelings get you down.
It's like summer changing to the cold of winter;
Day sliding down the dark side of night
And smiles fading into frowns.

Nothing is left to hope for
Your peaceful existence turns into a war
Of bitter agony and frustrations
Like good health giving way to a terminal disease.

When love is gone
It is hard for you to go on
Your whole spirit droops
Like a plant without roots.

You soon realize
Love is food to the body and soul
When you have it you must hold on to it.
If you don't have it . . .
You should pursue it.

## Let Me Go

You were there at a perfect time for me
To help heal a wounded spirit.
Then everything just happened,
As if planned by fate.
And now . . . it is too late.

It's an age old story of forbidden love;
One that was wrong right from the start.
I knew in the beginning it would happen;
Loving you would only break my heart.

The time would come when we would have to part.
I didn't want to face that possibility.
I thought our love affair would last forever;
There was no other way for it to be!

But now . . . confusing thoughts are clouding my mind.
Our times together . . . romantic? Yes . . .
Exciting? . . . you bet!
And yet . . . very frustrating,
Because those times always end too soon.

The hurt and pain when you are not there . . .
Too much . . . simply too much to bear.
It is something we both know
You will just have to let me go!

I know it will be rough
But a few stolen moments of love just aren't enough.
So give me a chance
To find romance

With someone who is free
To always be there for me.
So will you please . . . just let me go?

I keep hating
The time I spend waiting
Just to hear your voice when you call.
But more and more times it never happens at all.
However, I'm not ashamed
To feel the pain
Of loving you.

There is only one thing we can do
End it now . . . end all the pain.
The double life we live hurts too much.
This, we both know
So please . . . just let me go!

You say you love me
And think about me all the time
That's all in your mind
Still you are not with me
We can't be together when we want to be.
Can't you see . . .
    You must let me go!

Life will be empty without you
But somehow I'll make it through.
My feelings are going
Back and forth . . . to and fro . . .
Confused . . . hurting
Doubt . . . uncertain
So please . . . please . . . just let me go!

## Your Touch

Your gentle touch
  Means so much.
It makes me come alive
  With deep passion and thrive
  Like a thirsty desert flower
That has just had a spring shower.

Those feelings I had neatly tucked away so long
  Spring forth . . . so strong.
  You ignite the fire
  Bringing out my desire,
Filling me with emotion
      And deep devotion. . . .
Smooth . . . like a glass of vintage wine,
  Causing tingling sensations
  To run up and down my spine. . . .
Bursting forth into electrifying shocks
      All over my body.

You make me feel so special . . .
  So wanted and needed. . . .
Fulfilling the hunger of needing
  Someone to love me . . . to hold me
  And whisper into my ear
Words of caring that I love to hear.

We kiss . . .
    Exuding magic bliss
      Oh, so sweet . . .
Making me feel whole . . . complete
Then I look into your eyes
    That penetrate mine,
And I feel your love reach out to me each time.

We have a mutual feeling
	That sends us reeling
Into passionate ecstasy.
Nothing else matters . . . it's just you and me!

We share a deep love
	That no one can take from us
		We have no fears. . . .
It has stood the test through the years. . . .
	It is ours forever!

You feel my sorrow and hurt. . . .
	I'm your precious little "squirt."
You share my happiness and joy. . . .
	You are my darling "lover boy."

You are mine to hold. . . .
	To love and cherish
I'm yours until the end. . . .
You are my lover and my friend
		You say it all . . .
			In your magic touch!

## Memories

Memories . . .
    Drifting through my mind
    Like the soft petals of a rose . . .
    As a gentle breeze
    Scatters them in all directions
    Falling lightly upon green grass.
    Lying motionless—quietly
    Soaking up the warm sunshine
      of past joys.

Memories . . .
    Basking in the warmth
    Of each brilliant ray
    On times when no words
    Had to be spoken . . .
    Just a touch . . . a smile
    Or special look in our eyes
    Were telltale signs
    Of deep feelings of love
    Kindling the fires of passion.

Memories . . .
    Swinging back and forth
    Like the pendulum on a clock
    Unable to stop
    Remembering the dark shadows
    Creeping in . . . changing
    Our joy to sadness.
Desperately attempting to sift through
    What to hold on to
    And what to let go.

Memories . . .
    Clinging on in the deep crevices
    of my mind . . . marching all around
    Like little warriors
        Good and bad
        Happy and sad
    In battle with one another.

Memories . . .
    Haunting me night and day
    Every heartbeat
    Echoes the drumbeating rhythm
    Of my mind . . . marching all around
    Mixed thoughts and feelings
    Of joy, hurt, happiness, pain, and sorrow.

Memories . . .
    Where do I put them?
    Impossible to erase them
    All the memories
    Whatever they are
    Will be with me forever.
    With courage, I will face them.

## Your Love

Your love means so much to me.
It makes me feel complete.
Giving me such stability;
A love that can't be beat.

You give me courage when I'm afraid,
And praise me when I succeed.
You guide me in doing the things I dread.
Your love is all I need.

Whenever the dark shadows fall,
And I can't find my way;
You are there at my beck and call,
Always with the right words to say.

Your love for me is so strong,
That we seem to have become one.
You always know when something goes wrong,
Almost before it has begun.

I hope your love will always be
As strong as it is today.
And you will always be there for me
When I have lost my way.

# NATURE

## Close to Nature

Flowers bowing their heads in the gentle breeze,
Birds flitting about in the trees
Chirping a melodious song.
I can sit patiently all day long . . .
      So close to nature.

Bees humming from flower to flower,
The sun moving across the sky each passing hour,
The magic web being spun by a spider,
A mother cat sits with her kittens beside her . . .
      A splendid picture of nature.

A colony of ants building an ant hill,
Pigeons cooing on a window sill,
White cottony clouds float across a blue sky;
Then I hear a baby cry . . .
      Adding its sounds of nature.

A dog barking, chasing after a car,
Sounds of a chorus singing from afar.
Children's voices heard playing in the park
Mingling with the song of the lark . . .
      Making mixed sounds of nature.

Then crickets start singing their songs of love,
As well as the early morning dove.
Our heavenly Father surely must adore us,
To provide such a beautiful chorus . . .
      Through nature.

# A Lesson from the Squirrel

I was working in my flower bed one day,
When all of a sudden to my dismay
A squirrel was burying a nut in the dirt.
"Get out of here!" I yelled, "You little jerk."

I picked up a rock to hit him on the head,
But for some reason, changed my mind instead.
I could plainly see and began to take heed
He helped spread seeds around for all the trees we need.

He ran swiftly up a tree and looked back at me,
And started chirping furiously.
He seemed to be saying, "I'm a part of God's plan,
I help get things done, as well as man!"

I stood there and thought and had to agree,
Because it was clear and I could plainly see
He really wasn't such a jerk,
He was only helping to do God's work.

# Winter

Bleak, gray, and dreary,
Bare trees with gnarled branches
Gracefully bending their heads
As the wind whistles
A melody through them.
Sometimes the howling sound becomes fierce.

Soon the sky
Releases snowflakes that fly
In all directions—landing in heaps,
Changing the dull gray all around
Into a new dress of white glistening beauty,
With such grace and finesse.
'Tis the siege of winter.

Then the dark clouds break,
Sweeping across the sky.
Rays of sunshine peep through,
Falling upon the snowdrifts
With dancing magic,
Changing a gray winter day
Into a perfect view
Of a real live picture post card.
There is majestic beauty in winter!

## The Rose

A rose is a symbol of life;
    A mixture of beauty and strife.
The petals, radiant and sweet
    Representing all of life's good treats;
Love, good times and success . . .
    Joy, laughter, and happiness.

And then, there are the thorns
    That will prickle the life of every newborn.
But just as the thorns protect the rose,
    So do the thorns in life keep us composed
To face all of life's ups and downs;
    When pricked by a thorn we won't frown,

Because the beauties of life help to dispel
    All pain and hurt, and we strive to excel
To face life's challenges without fear
    Knowing that God is always near.
God created us, as well as the rose,
    What's best for us, He always knows.

## Free as a Bird

What if man could be
  Free as birds—
Sitting on a tree limb
  Singing a sweet melody.

Soaring through the air
  Or flitting in a bird bath—
    Splashing water everywhere.

Little bit by bit
  Uniquely building a nest;
    A home for their young,
And watching over them
    With such patience and care.

Singing through all kinds of weather,
  Happy and free of worry,
Because they know
  God will provide all they need.

Why can't we take heed
  And be—
    Free as a bird?

# The Master Artist

Gazing out the window that early morn,
I saw nature in all its glory.
Day was chasing away the dawn;
It was a display of a magical story.

The ground was covered with a blanket of snow.
Soft sounds of melting icicles and a hissing wind;
An early morning sun was all aglow
Causing all the winter colors to blend.

Bare branches on the old oak trees
Bent their heads from the weight of the ice.
Frozen pine branches were swinging in the breeze;
Glistening like diamonds all sparkling and nice.

God's nature, God's beauty, nothing could replace
The sunbeams dancing over the ice on the trees,
Appearing as Christmas lights blinking with such grace.
Bringing about a deep feeling of ease.

Suddenly a red bird from limb to limb flits.
Three little squirrels scamper over the snow.
Upon the fence a blue bird sits;
As if watching nature put on her show.

Man, through his efforts can duplicate
Nature's beauty in all its array.
But the Master Artist simply creates
Such beauty as seen on that winter day.

I, too, was watching the moving scene;
Thrilled, awed, with a smile on my face.
Knowing that the entire setting and theme,
Was the work of the Master Artist out there in space!


## My Flowers

I cherish the many precious hours
That I sit and meditate among my flowers.
I seem to have them everywhere,
So green and plush, responding to my care.

They are God's creation through me,
Expressing life, love, and beauty.
Giving me much to be proud of
By sharing my time, energy, and love.

Working with my flowers makes me feel calm.
When I'm in pain it's like a healing balm;
Soothing nerves and easing tension,
The pleasures derived are too many to mention.

There's a tremendous joy in watching them grow
Sometimes fast and sometimes slow.
They make me feel closer to God,
As He looks on and approves with a nod.

Flowers are used to express many feelings
Joy and love, sadness and healing.
But no matter, whatever the reason
They warm the heart in every season.

# God's Mysteries

O God, many things of nature I don't understand
But this I know, You are always in command.
Although scientists have tried to make things plain,
There are still so many things hard to explain.
However, I really would like to try,
So if You don't mind, may I ask You why?

So many stars, so far away,
How the night changes to day,
The moon following me around,
Where does the sun go when it goes down?

The endless sky that is so blue,
No artist can paint such a beautiful hue,
The rainbow hanging in the sky,
The fluffy clouds that go rushing by.

The rain that falls on hills and plains,
Bursting the seeds of flowers and grain,
Smoke trailing from rooftops far and near,
Where does it go when it disappears?

The billowy ocean waves that roar,
While high up above the seagulls soar,
Wind kissing my face, yet I cannot see;
Birds flying south so happy and carefree.

The beginning of a new life, domestic or wild,
A human mother giving birth to a child,
The unique life cycle of every living thing,
How do the flowers know when it is spring?

Everything that goes up must come down.
How a tiny seed bursts and grows through the ground?
How the planets move with such precision
Without ever having a collision?

Then there are earthquakes, storms, lightning, and
    thunder,
So puzzling and confusing and they make me wonder.
How do they know when to stop and when to start?
Then I realize that's where You take part.

You are so big and powerful, You are everywhere!
You created everything by speaking and it was there.
When everything was finished, You said it was good.
So it made no difference whether man understood.

O God, I have to face a fact that is worse,
There is so much I don't know about this vast universe.
So I won't worry about what I don't understand;
As long as I know it is in Your hands!

# The Beauty of a Sunset

While sitting in the stillness
Of the quiet evening breeze,
I watched the sun as it sank
Lower and lower behind the trees.

The tall shimmering shadows
Etched their way across a brook,
As the surrounding green grass
Took on a rich darker look.

A streak of soft fluffy clouds
Crept slowly over the sun
Changing into a rainbow of colors
Then merging into one.

The sun rays burst forth
Bathing the area in hues so bright
In such splendor and beauty,
As if defying the coming of night.

A glorious feeling came over me.
Because I knew God was close by.
Who else could paint such a picture
Up there in the sky?

## God's Glory

God's glory is everywhere
We look up into the heavens and it is there
Clouds, raindrops, snowflakes, blue sky
The birds and butterflies flying by.

We see it there in the moon and stars
Jupiter, Saturn, Mercury and Mars
And in all the other constellations
Are all a part of God's creation.

We look below and see much more
All that the green earth holds in store
The flowering plants and giant trees
Streams, brooks, river, and seas.

In beholding God's glory in the heavens and earth
We find it within us through our miraculous birth
Filled with thoughts, aspirations, and emotions
We give Him the praise in deep devotion.

# Nature's Dress

Nature is always at her best
As she changes into her seasonal dress.
All the beautiful colors seem to blend.
How she does it is hard to comprehend.

In winter everything is somewhat bare,
But there is enough green left to make us aware
That there is still plenty of life around;
Although leaves have fallen to the ground.

There is no match for her dress in spring;
Or the feeling of being so alive it brings,
As we watch colors burst forth with such splendor,
All feelings of lifelessness we'll have to surrender.

She takes on more colors as summer moves along.
Birds add more beauty to the scene with their song.
Flowers of red, pink, orange, yellow and white
Help make her dress a beautiful sight.

Autumn brings colors of a bright mixture
As if an artist painted the picture.
There is red, orange, brown, yellow, and gold
It is a wonderful sight to behold.

# The Ocean Waves

The ocean waves have a certain mystery
That is extremely hard to explain.
The churning and splashing so gracefully,
Like an old sweet song's refrain.

Yet there's a bit of turbulence in them,
Of which man is no match.
So care must be taken when we swim
Or the sea animals we try to catch.

The lapping of the waves against the shore
Is so calming it lulls you to sleep.
Falling into deep slumber more and more;
Peaceful dreams come, and are so sweet.

As you sit and watch the waves from a hill,
You are reminded of Christ's power.
When He spoke to them saying "Peace be still,"
And they subsided that very hour.

Whatever the mystery is, we can truly say
All of God's creation is unique.
The wind and the billows will obey,
Whenever the Master speaks!

## Autumn

The rustling of the leaves
As the wind blows through the trees
Quickly frees our minds
Of the hot summer we've just left behind.

There is a chill in the air
And for miles and miles everywhere
Nature clothes herself in a new dress,
One so beautiful words cannot express.

The leaves suddenly and magically
Take on colors so lovely to see;
As if some artist used paint and brush
To give them their colors so rich and plush.

This special time of year
Makes us know that God is near,
Changing all the colors before our eyes.
In His hands this magic lies.

# The Healing Waters

Walking along the beach in a lot of pain
As the ocean tide flapped against the shore,
The melody and rhythm caused me to remain.
Suddenly the pain was no more.

Burdened with a problem, no answers I could find.
I sat down beside a rippling brook.
The water flowing over the rocks eased my mind.
Suddenly ideas came and I knew where to look.

I needed the right words to say to a friend,
While I sat fishing on a quiet river bank.
I had no idea where I would begin;
Then suddenly my fishing line sank.

The ripples in the water began to spread;
Getting wider and wider and farther away.
As I watched, thoughts ran through my head.
I knew exactly what I wanted to say.

There is something about water that heals and calms
The innermost part of us
It is Jesus offering water as a healing balm.
In Him we can always trust.

# PEOPLE

# A Tribute to Senior Citizens

Old age has its drawbacks, but don't despair;
You belong to a group that is precious and rare.
Old things are priceless, we are told
Millions are spent on antiques, more precious than gold.

An old pair of shoes wears better than new.
It is said that aged wine is better, too.
So have no fears of growing old, everything is fine.
You're not just growing older, you're getting better all the
 time.

When we look at you we see a garden of flowers.
A rich mixture of beautiful living hours
That you have willingly shared with our youth.
Now today it is your moment of truth.

We see roses of kindness, patience and love;
Inspired by the blessings from God above.
But we can't have roses without some thorns;
And you've experienced many since the day you were
 born.

You have thorns of heartache, suffering, and pain.
And still some disappointments and struggles remain.
But the smell and beauty of the roses help you to bear
The problems in your life because others care.

We see petunias of courage and endurance,
Sunflowers of helpfulness as you gave assurance.
In helping so many youngsters reach their goal,
And all the young lives you helped to mold.

109

There are orchids of forgiveness, marigolds of caring;
Daisies of giving and gardenias of sharing.
On a fence are morning glories of thankfulness and grace
For all the hardships you had to face.

There are lilies of prayer growing everywhere.
And violets of Christian fellowship that you share.
But growing among the flowers, we see a few weeds;
However, God was there to always meet your needs.

You faced some weeds of hurt feelings and tears
But you found strength to overcome through the years.
You traveled rocky roads and valleys that were deep.
Some hot, dry deserts, and mountains that were steep.

Each of you has clocked a lot of mileage of living,
But there is a lot left, so keep on giving
Your love, time and energy as you continue to run this race.
Do not despair—you can do it with God's mercy and grace.

# The 20th Century Woman

The 20th Century woman . . .
    All sizes, races, colors and creeds . . .
    a new breed . . .
    An extension of women of old
    who have rocked the cradle of civilization,
    Carrying out old traditions—improving
    and adding on to them
    With dauntless courage.

The 20th Century woman . . .
    Emerging on the forefront of today's society
    Finding her rightful place on the world's stage,
    Playing her special role . . .
    In shaping and molding
    The civilization of tomorrow!

She has come a long way . . .
    From the drudgery of mere household chores
    and rearing a family
    To all facets of life in her community . . .
    the nation and the world!

The 20th Century woman . . .
    Making strides . . . Right beside
    Her male counterparts
    In politics, government, business, industry,
    Education, medicine, religion, technology
    She is blazing new trails
    Never attempted before
    Opening every possible door.
    Wherever man is . . . so is she!
    That's the way it should be!

The 20th Century woman
    Is made of the right stuff
    Just tough enough
    To fight for her rightful place
    When it is denied.

She is God's creation
    Man's helpmate . . . his equal
    Created to walk by his side;
    Not behind, and not being denied
    The right to fulfill her potential.

The 20th Century woman
    Is brave and courageous
    Her enthusiasm is contagious
    Spreading among others
    Giving them desires to move on
    Her willpower and determination are endless.
    She turns the word "no" around to "on" . . .
    Meaning on to greater goals
    And higher heights—with all her might!

She is intense—complex.
    No one can second guess her intentions. . . .
    Not to mention
    The sudden outburst of brilliant ideas
    Flowing through her keen mind,
    Seeking, searching, in her efforts to find
    Solutions to improve life for all humankind.

The 20th Century woman
    Is willing to listen to men
    But demands the right to be heard
    And get her two-cents' worth in.
    This right she will defend!

The 20th Century woman
    Likes to be her own person,
    But will stand by her man
    When the storms of life tear him apart,
    Because she has a heart
    Bigger than life itself;
    Holding so much love, compassion,
    Forgiveness, sharing, and caring for everyone else.

She is strong, yet tender and loving,
    Promotes peace and justice without pushing and
        shoving
    She is brave enough to go out on her own
    And make a home
    For her children,
    Working, struggling, and praying
    For their success.
    For them, she wants the best!

The 20th Century woman
    Plays many different roles
    All wrapped up in one body and soul . . .
    Mother, housewife, nurse, business woman,
    Counselor, teacher, religious advisor
    And on it goes—whatever person the occasion fits
    She is it!
    She is the hubcap of the family unit,
    Without her the family would disintegrate!

The 20th Century woman
    Has staying power.
    She is battered sometimes, but not beaten,
    Bent, but not broken,
    May give out, but never gives up.
    She is much like a teakettle

113

Although she may be up to her neck in hot water
She can still sing
Whatever the consequences may bring!

She may be criticized
    Often ostracized
    And sometime despised
    Because of her views and opinions,
    But she ignores negative predictions
    And holds on to her convictions.

The 20th Century woman
    Has praying power.
    She is in touch with her Creator every hour,
    Leans on Him for guidance,
    Has the faith to believe in Him—and herself
    When hope is dim.
    She does not reach decisions
    Through pressure, but through prayer.
    Has the patience to wait and not despair
    Keeps her hopes high,
    As she looks toward the sky,
    knowing God is still there.
    When she comes to the end of her rope
    She ties a knot and hangs on with hope;
    Or lets go—and lets God!

The 20th Century woman
    Often deserted and cast aside by man
    Sheds tears many times,
    But she clears her mind,
    She gets her act together,
    Braves the stormy weather

And moves on—searching
For a better life;
Rising above all the strife!

The 20th Century woman
　　Moving into the 21st Century
　　Ready to pass the torch on
　　To her descendants
　　With her heart filled with a song.

Generations to come
　　Will know that she was here,
　　And left a legacy
　　For them to live by and hold dear.

The 20th Century woman
　　Will leave her mark upon the pages
　　Of history behind
　　And her footprints
　　In the sands of time!

# The Minister's Wife

The minister's wife
Leads a rather lowly life.
She has to be strong,
In order to face the many wrongs

That are usually thrust upon him,
And the many times when hope is dim.
When nothing he does seems to be right,
As he tried to show his members the light.

She has to sit by and listen to complaints
Coming from the many so-called saints
Who have put themselves in high places.
And mumble and grumble with a scowl on their faces.

Often she sees the pain and hurt in his eyes.
Many times she slips away and cries.
And prays fervently to the Almighty God,
To give him the strength to do the job

That He has called up on him to do
No matter how many heartaches he has to go through.
So she stands by him through thick and thin,
Knowing God will help him triumph in the end.

She is strengthened as she sees a ray of hope beam.
And feels good about being part of a team
That God has assigned a special job to do.
And knows He will always see them through.

## Portrait of a Minister

He is God's servant—
    Ordained to carry out His will
    Striving each day to guide and instill
    The teachings of God's word and his mission fulfill.

He is God's hands—
    Reaching out to touch some twisted mind
    Hoping, praying and urging them to find
    A better way to live with all humankind.

He is God's eyes—
    That see the blight of hatred and sin.
    And cries out for mercy for a friend,
    For their sinful ways to mend.

He is God's ears—
    That hear the cries of his fellowman
    Works hard to help them understand
    How to fit into God's plan.

He is God's feet—
    That always walk the extra mile
    To visit the sick and lonely and spend a while
    Telling them everyone is God's special child.

He is God's heart—
    Filled with forgiveness when others do him wrong.
    One that is always filled with a song
    Of praise and thanksgiving all day long.

He is God's love—
    Given freely expecting nothing in return:
    Deep down within he lets it burn
    To light someone's way and of the Savior learn.

    He really seems to be God's mind,
    Because it takes a very special kind.
    And we are sure there is no doubt,
    Our minister is the one we're talking about.

## A Call for Help

A loud ringing of the phone one early morn
Brought a scowl to my face and filled me with scorn.
"I wonder who it is," I mumbled angrily,
"Why can't everybody just let me be?"

"Hello," I said in a dry tone of voice.
"Praise the Lord," my pastor shouted, "time to rejoice."
"How are you, Reverend?" I managed to say.
"Fine, dear sister, but I need your help today."

"How can I help?" I asked all wide-eyed.
"I'm burdened this morning," slowly he replied,
"I need a little lift. I'm really feeling down."
*Oh my*, I thought, *he's turning things around*.

"Take just a moment," he said, "of your precious time,
And say a prayer for me, then I will be fine."
I was somewhat startled and quickly asked, "Now?"
"Yes," he pleaded, "so may we bow?"

My lips parted and the words began to flow,
And suddenly a warm feeling made my heart all aglow.,
I always thought I needed my pastor to pray for me
But the tables were turned, I could plainly see.

The pastor was just human like everybody else,
Perhaps he prayed for others, and forgot about himself,
I was glad he called on me to do that noble deed,
There was a feeling of joy, and it filled my need.

## The Complainer

Some people can walk into a room
And immediately cast a shadow of gloom.
Not a gory detail will they miss.
They complain about that and complain about this.

Their health is in the worst shape it's ever been.
You can't seem to get one word in.
Hour after hour they will complain
Over and over about their aches and pain.

They move on to the weather being too hot or too cold;
And about making a bad deal on something they sold.
How they can't seem to make ends meet,
Although they work hard and have tired feet.

They don't care if you have problems, too,
And can't tell them what they should do.
When they finally leave you're glad they're gone,
Because you are tired of hearing their sad song.

Instead of people always complaining
They should be thankfully proclaiming
All of the blessings God showers down.
They should smile with joy instead of frown.

Don't be guilty of doing the same.
It is always so easy to complain.
Think of all the blessings you have had.
The good will always outweigh the bad.

## A Good Teacher

She has tried over and over again,
But just can't seem to get through
To those blank faces grimacing with strain;
And wonders what else can she do!

She knows there has to be a way
To make the difficult clear;
And starts all over again, come what may,
Without any doubt or fear . . .

That if she gives it one last try,
The results will be a success.
Her expectations are always high,
Because she knows she is giving her best.

Joy fills her heart as the payoff comes,
When she sees the light in each student's face.
She is sure another battle has been won
And has the urgent desire to embrace . . .

Each anxious student in her class,
Who shows they now understand;
Knowing the knowledge she imparted will last
And they'll always do the best they can.

She praises her students for each little success;
Her patience will run out, never.
She feels if they are able to pass life's test,
Through them she'll live on forever!

# Will Humans Become Extinct?

Everything is so impersonal sometimes I think
Humans will eventually become extinct.
Machines are taking over in every way;
From what I can see they are here to stay.

You pick up the phone to call a friend,
And hear a machine on the other end.
You call to make a reservation when leaving town
Then you're told to wait, the computers are down.

You have a problem that you need to discuss,
But end up listening to a machine and a lot of fuss.
Frustration and despair take over your mind,
Because personal communication is hard to find.

Numbers are taking the place of names,
In business and social life they are the same.
A social security number identifies us,
Securing one by everybody is a must!

Numbers identify us in most places.
No one seems to care about human faces.
We are just like objects being shuffled about.
I wonder how our race will eventually turn out.

People say you're crazy when you talk to yourself
But what must you do, there is nobody else?
Machines are okay when you don't have a choice,
However, there are times when you need to hear a human
    voice.

# A Profile of Good Leaders

Leadership ability must constitute
Many strong qualities or attributes.
First, one must follow before they can lead.
It helps to provide the experience they need.

Good strong leaders are always understanding
Give guidance without being demanding.
Don't feel the need to be in the limelight
And that nobody else can do anything right.

Patience is a quality they must possess
If they expect their leadership to be blessed.
Have the courage to admit when they are wrong,
This trait will help to make them strong.

They know how to take criticism with grace;
Have the willingness to always face
All the rough punches coming their way
By knowing just the right words to say.

A lot of loyal followers they can win
Just by showing that they are a true friend.
Give a pat on the back for a job well done,
Recognize the accomplishments of everyone.

Give praise and credit to others when it's due,
Let them know they are important too.
Know how to give them a push in the right direction
Use diplomacy and tact in making corrections.

They must be flexible, at the same time firm
If respect from others they want to earn.
Can't be one way today, and another tomorrow,
Because that only brings about a lot of sorrow.

When feelings are hurt they always forgive
Have a heart filled with love that helps them live
As shining examples for all to see
The faith and hope they impart so willingly.

Most of all they know how to pray
For guidance to help show them the way
To deal with others through humility and peace
So that all dissension and confusion will cease.

They depend on God to bless, sustain and guide
Know He will always be by their side.
And they never, ever try to do a job
Without first being led by God!

# The Kindred Souls

They were all there—from everywhere
The kindred souls came together
From the far corners of some place else.
All shapes, sizes and colors . . .
In wheelchairs, on walking canes
All races and nationalities
As one big happy family.

The kindred souls
With the same hearts and minds
Reaching out to one another.
Their eyes pierced each other's;
Thought waves connected like magnets.
The multitude of creativity smoldered . . .
Just waiting to burst forth like fireworks
On the Fourth of July!

Ideas waiting to be born
Were hanging on the tips of their brains.
There was a mutual sharing of these ideas.
Even before speaking thoughts were interlocking
With the thoughts of many!

The kindred souls
Came together for one common goal,
To express and share feelings of the soul.
Such beautiful people
Representing God's greatest gift . . .
A love for the expression of beauty—deep and real . . .
Feelings and emotions of the heart
Feelings running deep, quiet, calm,
Yet a bit of turbulence at the same time.

There was evidence of God-like thoughts.
Seemingly being able to know
Not only how many seeds found in an apple,
But how many apples are in a seed.
The gift of being able to look at the simple things
In simple surroundings
And to write about much more
Than meets the human eye . . .
Expressions of the heart and soul.

The kindred souls
Whose conversations were filled with
Such deep emotions . . .
Tears were shed,
Spirits were lifted
Lasting friendships were made
Bonds were solidified
Never to be broken!

The kindred souls
Together—a special breed
Filling a special need
For themselves
And a world of others.

The kindred souls
Were all poets!

# One Common Denominator

You may travel the nations wide,
And people of all descriptions meet,
In cities, towns or countryside,
Public gatherings or just on the street.

Somehow it never seems to fail,
There is a common denominator in those we meet,
As if God went to great detail
To make it an exceptional feat.

While traveling in a plane high up in the air
So frustrated, lonely, tired, and afraid
Seated between two people from I knew not where
When suddenly one of them said . . .

"Hi, I'm Millie, what is your name?"
Then I politely told her mine.
To my amazement our interests were the same.
From that moment on everything was fine.

Talking with the other one it was revealed
That we, too, held a common bond.
So high up in the air our friendship was sealed.
Memories of them will always be fond.

One was a poet just like me
And we were going to the same convention.
The common floodgates opened making us feel free
The joys of our meeting are too many to mention!

The other one was a widow and so was I.
This information just seemed to come out.
Going over the sad memories made us want to cry,
But we got strength from each other, no doubt.

This one experience made me know
That we are not strangers as I recall,
Because no matter where we may go,
There is a common denominator in all.

## "John Q. Public"

There's a guy out there that people try to please.
He's old John Q. Public who stretches what he sees.
In his subtle way he keeps them on the run.
They don't dare let him know about the things they've
    done.

He's on every corner watching the moves they make.
If he catches them doing wrong they've made a big mistake.
The news is quickly leaked to the old grapevine
And spreads like wildfire with fuel combined.

It's sad that people worry about old John Q.
When God also sees everything they do.
They should be concerned about what He'll have to say,
When they have to face Him on that judgment day!

# SPIRITUAL INSPIRATION

# God Speaks

God speaks to us in many ways,
If we only take time to listen . . .
By communing with nature throughout our days
We can see all His wonders glisten.

He speaks to us through the flowers that bloom;
The silvery moonlight and twinkling stars.
Lifting our spirits, banishing all gloom;
Soothing hurts and healing scars.

We can hear His voice in the thunder,
And the splashing of the ocean waves.
We marvel at the magnificent wonder
Of streams trickling through underground caves.

We hear Him speaking through the birds that sing,
The robin, the lark, and the mourning dove;
That renew our hearts in early spring
Singing praises of His steadfast love.

The whispering wind blowing through the trees
Is a most calming and thrilling sound to hear.
And the crisp rustling of the leaves,
Tells us He is always near.

When the lightning is flashing across the sky
The ominous clouds are dark and large,
We have no need to fear or sigh,
God is telling us He is still in charge!

# The Best Medicine

A lot of our ills are self-inflicted,
Because our spiritual diet is restricted.
We nibble at faith and fail to have hope,
Our vision for surviving becomes limited in scope.

We search and search looking far and wide;
Hoping to find something that can be prescribed
That will ease all our fears and doubts
And all our discontent will be blotted out.

The best medicine for deep depression
Is to find a quiet place and have a prayer session.
God will be there to make the burden light.
Depression will vanish and the way will be bright.

If our ailment is an unexpected sorrow
God's word is the best medicine; things will be better
      tomorrow.
When we use the proper dosage, sorrow disappears
An end will come to all of our tears.

Sometime anger and bitterness consume our minds
So overwhelming that we strive to find
Some kind of medicine that spells relief,
Before we become responsible for a lot of grief.

Our spiritual diet should be filled with hope and faith.
When we have these ingredients, we'll never have to wait
For God's words to sink into our hearts.
Our ills will be over before they start.

# Finding God

Some skeptics find it hard
To believe there is a God.
They may ask how do we know.
We can easily tell them where to look or go.

It is so sad they can't see Him,
Because their spiritual vision is so dim.
People like this are so self-centered
In their minds, thoughts of others have never entered.

If you are such a person looking for God;
You would like to see Him, and have looked hard
In your own little narrow space;
My friend, you just need to look in the right place.

Jesus tells us in a special way
Where we can find Him each and every day.
He tells us He is among the hungry and the poor
All you have to do is open your door.

He's among the homeless, sick, lonely and neglected.
Just look to Him; your steps will be directed
To look where people are; those who are in need of love.
And you can share blessings from God up above.

They may be in crowded cities; all kinds you can meet.
And a likely place to look is the house down the street.
We can find God wherever people are,
So there is no excuse, you don't have to go far.

God is in the midst of everything and place.
You can be aware of His unchanging grace.
If you still have difficulty, then look to Calvary.
There on a cross is God dying for you and me!

# Count Your Blessings

Count your blessings before you complain.
Don't let all that God has taught you go down the drain.
Be grateful to Him for His healing touch.
Be thankful for a little, and He will give you much.

When you complain about eating the same food all the
      time,
Think about all the people standing in a soup line.
You can't stand your mortgage interest rate being so high,
But the street people's home is the ground and the sky!

You're tired of your old clothes, they're out of style.
For those old clothes some people would walk a mile.
It annoys you when asked to make a contribution
To some worthwhile charity institution.

You say your aching legs and feet are hard to bear;
Think of the people without legs in a wheelchair.
Your world comes to an end when you have a little cold.
Have you thought about patients in nursing homes
      growing old?

Bills take all our paychecks, you feel like you've been
      robbed.
But what about those people who don't even have a job?
You go to church on Sunday but hate to pay your dues;
Hating to go to work on Monday, you cry and sing the
      blues.

Stop and count your blessings when nothing seems right.
Those brief moments will shed a lot of light . . .
On all the good things God is doing for you.
You will stop complaining and be more thankful, too.

# Opportunity

Opportunity knocks on everyone's door
It may be in disguise.
Since we are never sure we know,
Examining it will be wise.

If you hurry, and turn it away
You may miss out on a chance
To reach a goal you desired,
Because you merely gave it a glance.

It may come in the form of a tragedy.
And it is very hard for you to understand,
That some good can come out of it.
Because it is just a part of God's plan.

It could be in the form of an interruption
That briefly interferes with your plans.
You look at it as an unwanted nuisance
That always seems to be on hand.

It may come as a sudden disaster
That erupts and destroys your progress.
You feel that you can not handle it,
But later find it was the door to success.

There's no way you would think a form of illness
Could be an opportunity for something good.
But needless to say, sometimes it brings
Something to our lives that nothing else could.

When disguised opportunity knocks on your door
Take some time to think it through.
Don't ever send it away in haste,
It may be the best thing that ever happened to you!

## Jesus Needs Us

Jesus was forever borrowing
Although everything belonged to Him.
He was showing the lowly and sorrowing
How to keep His light from growing dim.

He borrowed the stable in which He was born
As the world waited for a king,
Two thousand years ago on Christmas morn,
Still today for which all people sing.

A boat was borrowed from which He preached
The Holy Word instructing all mankind,
Of the knowledge and wisdom until they reached
The status of a Christlike mind.

He borrowed two fish and five loaves of bread
And fed thousands in the hungry crowd.
Had baskets of scraps left over instead;
Easing their hunger, they gave thanks with heads bowed.

A donkey was borrowed for His triumphal procession
Into Jerusalem on that fateful day;
As people cried out hosanna in their confession
That He was king of kings, come what may.

He instituted the sacrament of holy communion
With His disciples in a borrowed upper room;
To teach them to come together in spiritual union;
He knew He would be leaving them soon.

He borrowed Simon of Cyrene's strong back
To help Him carry the old rugged cross,
As He struggled along stumbling in His tracks
To die for a world of sinners who were lost.

At last He was buried in a borrowed tomb,
But on the third day He rose.
Saving us from the devil, death and doom.
This truth every Christian knows!

Jesus doesn't have to borrow anything,
But He still needs our help today,
In spreading His gospel as Savior and King
And helping to show others the way.

He needs us to fill some special place.
To touch some life that no one else can.
We are not just here to fill an empty space,
But to give help to our fellowman.

## A Mind in Bondage

A mind against changes and new ideas,
Always sensing trouble before it appears.
A mind that is centered on one's self,
Refusing to consider anyone else
        Is a mind in bondage.

A mind that holds grudges against a brother
And blots out forgiveness toward one another.
Closes out love and holds on to hate,
Claims it can never make a mistake
        Is a mind in bondage.

A mind that thinks negatively about everything,
To disappointments, failures, it always clings.
Never feeling it can ever find success
By making a start and doing its best
        Is a mind in bondage.

Start today to set your mind free.
Give it a chance to grow and to be
Flexible, courageous, confident and complete,
Striving for success, never giving in to defeat . . .
        No longer in bondage!

## Grasp the Moment

Your world comes crashing down like a huge boulder.
Taking you by surprise landing on your shoulders.
You cry out "O Lord, this can't be happening to me!"
Because the reason for such a happening is so hard to see.

Grasp the moment to turn to God in prayer.
It just may be His way to show you that He cares.
He never promised all your skies would be blue,
But He did promise He would always be there for you!

Nothing is ever as bad as it seems,
And you can't believe in all your wildest dreams
That you will be able to turn things around
By grasping the moment, answers can be found.

Let the boulders come no matter how large.
With God by your side you can always take charge.
So grasp each moment as the days go by.
You can turn disaster into triumph if you try.

## This, Too, Shall Pass

It's a dark day in my life.
Fear pierces my heart like a knife,
But I realize it won't last;
So I whisper "This, too, shall pass."

The pain is so hard to bear.
Nobody ever seems to care.
But my faith I must hold fast;
For I know this, too, shall pass.

Dark clouds hover overhead;
Blurring my vision, making me afraid.
Ugly dark shadows are being cast,
But I'm sure this, too, shall pass.

The dancing lightning in the sky
Makes my courage and determination die.
The roaring thunder begins to blast,
But God assures me this, too, shall pass.


## The Master Teacher

God is the Master Teacher
Who needs no diploma or degree
To help us learn all the attributes,
And gives us all this for free.

He teaches us patience
Through life's ups and downs.
And how our work on earth
In heaven, leads to a crown.

Through all of our successes
He teaches us humility.
And helps us to realize
That it's the best way to be.

There is no greater lesson learned
Than charity and love,
That adds stars to our crown
In that heavenly place above.

Through many trials and tribulations,
A lesson in faith is learned.
As we struggle on in spite of failures,
A reward of success can be earned.

He teaches us how to forgive
The sins committed against us,
And always how to humble ourselves,
To earn our fellowman's trust.

Endurance is a needed trait
That we must learn from Him,
When our way gets dark and hopeless
And our chances of success look slim.

We learn to show our thankfulness
By praising His Holy Name.
For He is responsible for all our success,
Whether it is fortune or fame.

Sometimes success goes to our head,
And long-suffering He must apply
To teach us that He is still in charge,
And we can never pass Him by.

We can face life with courage
And always pass the test.
For the lessons that He teaches us,
Because He always knows what's best.

## Then Comes the Morning

The shadows of night fall around you;
Fears and anxieties are magnified.
You feel there is no way you can make it through.
Your hopelessness can not be denied. . . .
 But then comes the morning!

One thing that is certain
As our nerves we try to calm;
The pain gets worse as night draws its curtains,
But have no fear, there is a balm . . .
 When the morning comes!

The darkness is filled with restless sleep
And nightmares invade your dreams.
You lie awake and count sheep.
You're so frustrated you want to scream. . . .
 But then comes the morning!

For some reason, I don't know why,
The morning always brings relief;
Giving the hope and courage to try
To find solutions for all our grief . . .
 When the morning comes!

# Pressing on to the Finish Line

Life is like a marathon.
The whistle blows and the race is begun.
You start running with all your might
On the road of life until the race is won.

Sometimes the running slows down a bit.
And you stop to rest for a while.
Then you get up and start out again,
Struggling steadily, mile after mile.

The sun beams down on your head,
And sweat rolls off your face.
But you can't stop—you must keep going
To make it to the end of the race.

The rain begins to fall and soaks your clothes.
You feel all soggy and wet.
It makes you uncomfortable, but you can't stop. . . .
You haven't reached the finish line yet.

Through the storms of life you must keep running,
Although you change your pace sometime
No matter what happens along the way
The race isn't over until you reach the finish line.

# Weathering the Storms of Life

The hurricane of life is churning
And thunder begins to roll.
Troubles gather like dark clouds.
Fear begins to take its toll.

Nothing is going as you planned.
Misfortunes, like lightning, strike everywhere,
Destroying all the confidence you had;
Leaving you filled with despair.

Problems pile up like heaps of snow,
And you struggle to dig your way out.
But a tornado of setbacks starts to whirl
Tossing your endurance and optimism about.

Your willpower spins like a cyclone.
The icy cold reality penetrates your mind.
Giving up seems to be the best thing to do,
Because help is so hard to find.

Perhaps, my friend, you have forgotten
The source of all your help.
So turn to God in humble prayer.
His promises He has always kept.

He will help you through the storms of life.
Turn all your burdens over to Him,
The darkness, the struggles, and all the strife;
The light of hope will no longer be dim.

## Endless Love

It was in existence
   long before the beginning of time . . .
The endless love . . . filled with all
   the right ingredients . . .
   long suffering, truth, meekness, kindness,
   endurance and hope . . .
Has trickled down through the ages
   from one generation to another.

The endless love . . . something the human
   mind finds hard to fathom . . .
How it can bring so much joy,
   yet bring pain and suffering!

It is trampled under the evil feet
   of hatred, prejudice, deception, and sin,
   abused, and misused . . .
But it always rises again . . .
   shakes the dirt off and flourishes . . .
   shining through, better and stronger
   than before!

The endless love . . . scales mountains high
   melting the snowcapped peaks of fear . . .
   warming heart and soul.
It spans oceans wide . . . and levels
   valleys deep
Breaks down barriers between lovers,
   families, friends, and nations
   of the world.

It is color-blind . . . looks beyond the
    outside and sees the heart
    and all that it holds.

The endless love . . . brought a Savior
    to set us free.
It walked the hot dusty roads of Galilee . . .
    spreading among all people.
Its power, mercy and forgiveness
    sustained civilizations.

The endless love . . . went to the cross
    and died to save a race that was lost . . .
    but rose again with power
    over death and sin . . .
    setting all mankind free
It will go on and on. . . . endlessly
    throughout eternity!

## The Door to My Lips

I'm careful about the door to my lips
I guard what passes through;
Making sure I let nothing slip
That will ever be offensive to you.

It is easy when the door is wide open
And my thoughts are not carefully planned
Uncaring words can be spoken
And others may not understand.

So I make sure my brain is in gear
Before I open my lips' door,
Then I will never have to fear
Speaking the wrong words anymore.

## The Harbors of the Mind

The mind . . . like the ocean
Is vast and mysterious
Thoughts . . . like the thousands
Of living things . . . come alive
Grow and thrive.

Ships . . . loaded with knowledge
Float in and out of the mind
Producing commodities of every kind.

Like the ocean . . . there is a harbor
To guard against what comes in
And what goes out.

You are the harbor master
It is your choice,
To open the harbor, or leave it closed.
It is left up to you to be in control
Of what comes and goes
Through the harbors of your mind.


## Reality Is Sweeter than the Dream

Life deals you a sudden blow;
All your hopes and dreams
Are shattered.
Everything that mattered
To you has vanished
Like a dense fog breaking up
When the warm sunshine pushes through.

You don't know what to do
Your future . . . totally out of reach it seems
Beyond time, beyond reality, beyond dreams.
But there is a course that you can take
To turn things around.
In Him new hope can be found.

Jesus is there to lend a helping hand
You can begin again
Your dream can become a reality
And reality is much sweeter than the dream!

## Life Is Not a Rehearsal

An entire lifetime can be wasted
Making preparations to live it.
We spend the time scheming,
Storing up wealth and dreaming.

Of the big moment becoming a reality
When we can skip down
The yellow brick road
To the land of our dreams
And live happily ever after!

Not so . . . life is to be lived now . . .
Now is the only time we have.
Each moment is so precious.
Rehearsing it to live tomorrow
Can only bring grief and sorrow.

Life is not a rehearsal for living
It is only a brief moment in time. . . .
Like a blade of grass . . .
That is cut down . . . withers and dies so fast.
Our tracks are blown away
By the dusty winds of time. . . .
To be no more!

Each moment of every day
Should be spent living
Life to its fullest
Loving and giving
Of our energy and time
To fulfill God's purpose for our being here!

We must not let life pass by
While we are getting ready to live it
But cram all the living we can
Into every precious minute,
Because life is not just a rehearsal for living!

## A Love Affair with Christ

Nothing can be more beautiful . . .
A love affair with Christ . . .
Pure and everlasting . . . agape love
Far above any love between humans
All given without a price!

Nothing physical, sordid or degrading
A spiritual love that looks beyond
Our faults and shortcomings
Even forgiving our sins against Him
And our fellowman . . . over and over again!

There are no separations and divorces
Because He stops loving us.
No court cases for property settlements
And custody battles . . . no fuss.
He is with us forever . . . day and night
No matter where we abide
He is always by our side.

His love will never cease
He tucks us in each night to sleep in peace
Watching over us. . . .
Protecting us from danger and harm
If we hurt He cradles us in his loving arms.
Holds our hand . . . because He understands.

150

He owns everything
And with us shares this wealth
Bears our suffering and pain
Restores and nurses our bodies back to good health.

He provides us with the food
Of eternal life with His body and blood.
Because of His mighty protecting hand
We can dwell in safety. . . .
He guards us and defends us
From the assaults of the evil one
Who is always near devouring throughout the land.

He gives us peace that passes all understanding
A peace that is complete. . . .
Making worry and anxiety obsolete.
His love is so strong
It never diminishes when we do wrong . . .
Loving us even when we are
Mean, stiff-necked, disobedient and unlovable!

The best part of this love affair . . .
We can call on Him anytime through prayer.
The lines of communication are never busy . . .
And we are never put on hold.
He's a terrific listener and always answers.
Supplying our needs with blessings untold.

No matter how much
Anyone else may love us
Their love can never touch
Or measure up to Christ's steadfast love.
It led him to the cross
To give his life for us
That our love affair would not be lost.

The endless love affair will go on
Even after death
When this life ends,
A new one begins
With Him in the beautiful place
He has prepared for us
To continue our love affair
Throughout eternity!

## Check the Ears of Your Heart

When silent voices are crying out,
But you don't seem to hear.
Your heart's ears are impaired, no doubt,
And the voices are not so clear.

Turn your thoughts deep down within,
And check the ears of your heart.
The message will get through and begin
To move you to do your part . . .

In reaching out, to some crying voice,
And meeting one's urgent need.
Your heart will gladly rejoice
That you have taken heed . . .

To God's calling in fulfilling His plan
In meeting the needs of some crying voice
By giving them a helping hand
Then God above will rejoice.

# Changes

We look forward to changes with anticipation,
At the same time with certain dread . . .
Of some undesirable situation
That makes us somewhat afraid.

We are like young eagles in their secure nest,
Who are afraid to try their wings.
But the mother eagle knows what is best
And pushes them out no matter how they cling.

Just as the eaglets would never fly
Were they not pushed out of the nest;
God brings changes that we may try
To soar spiritually and pass His test.

We need not have undue fear
When changes come unexpectedly.
God has assured us He is always near,
No matter how great the change may be.


# Tranformed by the Master's Touch

We were nothing;
    Just an idea in the Master's mind;
    No shape, size or form . . .
    Nothing!

Everything that is was nothing
    Just an idea in the Master's mind.
    No shape, size or form . . .
    Nothing!

And then He spoke!
Each day of the miraculous creation
  He spoke . . .
And all that nothingness
  Became something good
    And perfect.

But something was missing
  And He created man;
Then evil and sin began!
From one generation to another
Sin was passed on
The human race needed help!

A heart full of love
For fallen mankind
Brought us a Savior
To take all sin upon His shoulders.

The black hearts of humankind
No longer needed to search to find
A way out of darkness

Just the Master's touch
Can transform us into sparkling
Gems of Christian souls

All we need
  Is to take heed
And be transformed
  By the Master's touch!

# Jesus Is the Quarterback

Some feel that they can plan their lives
From the beginning until the end;
But will run into snags along the way,
And trouble around every bend.

They must realize life is like a game,
And no matter what anyone says,
Jesus is the quarterback
And He calls all the plays.

They try to go in one direction
Finding that way is blocked.
It would be easier to ask for guidance.
All they have to do is knock

On the door of their heart where Jesus is
And wait for the play He calls.
Life would be so simple
And more successful for us all.

## Adventures of Each New Day

As we begin each new day
It's like going on a safari far, far away.
There will be loads of surprises in store.
We may encounter disappointments, heartaches, and
 much more.

There'll be new changes we'll have to face
As we move around from place to place.
Danger and disaster may be lurking near,
But God will be with us and we need not fear.

We'll meet some jungle animals along the way,
As we continue our journey through the day.
We should be armed with a lot of faith and hope,
So we won't find ourselves at the end of our rope.

The old jungle lion of malice and greed
May get in our path and slow down our speed.
He'll be waiting in the shadows so he can devour
Our accomplishments and progress hour after hour.

The snake of deceit will be there to sneak
Upon our trail before we can speak.
And if we aren't careful we'll be taken in
To trust someone we thought was a friend.

The elephant of unforgiveness will never forget,
Minor misunderstanding and make us regret
All the mistakes we made in the past.
We'd like to put them behind, but they seem to last.

The tiger of confusion keeps everyone at odds,
To survive all this we'll surely need God
To stay by our side and keep us in control.
And let peace and understanding be our goal.

So when our adventure ends at the close of the day,
We should be able to sit down and say,
"Thanks, Lord, for protecting me in that jungle out there.
I'll never be afraid because I know You care!"

## God's Team

In our daily walk of life,
There are so many different teams.
Everyone is extremely anxious
To make theirs the best it seems.

There are football, basketball, and baseball
Just to name a few;
But what are your concerns about God's team,
One that will always pay off for you?

Try making a touchdown by giving your service.
Run fifty yards for a friend.
Don't stop until you reach the goal post.
When there're broken relations to mend.

Kick a field goal for extra points,
When you're offside in carrying your load.
Never be guilty of interference and holding
Someone back on life's twisting road.

Take advantage of free shots at success
When God willingly offers them to you.
Lay up points in the basket.
Avoid personal fouls 'til the game is through.

Never find yourself traveling too fast;
Pushing and shoving those in your way.
You'll only be penalized for your misdeeds
In the game of life we play.

Hit a homerun for a fallen friend
Who has struck out on his luck.
Some day a foul ball may come your way,
And you'll find that you are stuck.

Sometimes your mind's bases are loaded
And you run wildly into left field.
The umpire's call is not in your favor,
All your efforts have brought no yield.

You have to go back to bat again.
So keep your eyes on the pitcher's mound.
And you can hit all life's problems head on.
With God's help, strength can be found.

So why not join God's team
Before it is too late?
You can run life's race over hurdles,
And always make it to homeplate.

# Invest in Heaven

Man makes financial investments
In order to strike it rich.
He becomes obsessed in beating the odds,
Right or wrong, he doesn't care which.

He spends most of his life
Building up huge bank accounts.
Acquiring mountains of material things
In extremely large amounts.

His worth is considered by how much he owns.
Nobody seems to care about his soul;
So everybody struggles to make investments,
And stores up silver and gold.

Sad to say, he never seems to have enough,
But no matter how much he is worth,
Being greedy for wealth is a lost cause,
When he dies he takes nothing from this earth.

It behooves all of us to reevaluate
And decide whatever is best.
If we intend to spend eternity with God,
Heaven is the place we should invest.

So instead of snatching and grabbing here on earth,
We should send up some payments every day.
The Scriptures tell us the interest is great.
Investing in heaven brings the best pay.

## Hold on to Your Dreams

If you fantasize a lot, it's okay
Your fantasies can become a reality one day.
They are seeds planted in your heart
From them answers to your dreams may start.

Things may not move smoothly day after day,
But don't let despair get in the way.
Keep your thoughts running in a steady stream,
No matter what happens hold on to your dreams.

If there are setbacks when you make a start,
Never mind, all that is a part
Of the process of reaching your goal
Each pitfall plays an important role.

Nothing ventured is nothing gained.
There are many other options that remain.
Remember God is with you, on Him you can lean,
No matter what happens hold on to your dream.

Just keep your eyes on the prize,
Don't be reluctant to fantasize.
Success is not as impossible as it may seem,
So no matter what happens hold on to your dream.

# Spring Cleaning of the Soul

When life seems to be holding you down,
Instead of a smile, you're wearing a frown.
You're finding fault in everybody else,
It's time to take a good look at yourself.

Everything is wrong—nothing goes right;
Your future is dim instead of bright.
You find it impossible to reach your goal,
It's time for a spring cleaning of the soul.

Excess baggage is cluttering up your mind.
Take a good look, you'll find rubbish of every kind.
All the little stuff that you've been pushing inside
Is coming to the surface and you can no longer hide.

Deep within you are cobwebs of discontent
That change your disposition to something you never
    meant.
There is a lot of dust of dissatisfaction and greed;
Showing thanks for what you have is all you really need.

You are holding on to some old bitterness of the past.
Sweep them up, throw them out and be free of them at last.
There's mudslinging, grumbling, criticisms, and blame
For things that are upsetting when you, yourself have done
    the same.

Crawling inside you are grub worms of jealousy and hate.
You must find a way to kill them before it is too late.
You are plagued with dirty thoughts of filth, grime, and sin
That are so overwhelming you don't know where to begin.

The only possible perfect place is right there in your
　　heart.
Now, this day, this hour, is the best time to start.
The weight on your mind will be lifted and you can reach
　　your goal,
When you finally have done a spring cleaning of the soul.

Replace all the evil thoughts and rubbish with forgiveness
　　and love.
God will send His blessings to you from above,
Blessings that will be more precious than gold.
You'll be glad you did a spring cleaning of the soul.

# The Hands of Christ

His strong hands reached out and touched
The meek and lowly who needed strength so much.

His clean hands did no sinful deeds,
Always doing good and supplying others' needs.

His busy hands carried out His Father's will,
Before the time came to die upon Calvary hill.

His open hands said, "Come unto me
I will give you rest and set you free."

His praying hands in our behalf interceded,
To ask help from the Father whenever it was needed.

His blessing hands reached out to heal
Those who were sick, or to provide a meal.

His pierced hands showed the sacrifice He made,
The blood He shed for us and the debt He paid.

Oh, if our hands could be half as good,
Carrying out God's will as we should;
And remembering all His suffering and pain.
The price He paid will not have been in vain.

# God's Love Letter

The Bible is God's love letter
We should strive to understand it better.
It tells us just how much He loves us
And in His word we should always trust.

We learn from it all the promises He makes
And all that He has, and will do for our sake.
We should have faith and only believe
His steadfast love we will receive.

This love letter holds everything we need
The words found there will our souls feed
To grow and develop according to His plan
If we just read this letter we'll understand.

## The Brightest Light of All

He merely spoke and there was light,
Then all the darkness was gone,
Responding to His wondrous might
To give light that goes on and on.

Light . . . God's wonderful light . . .
Where would we be without it?
The sun, the moon, and stars so bright,
It's awesome just to think about it.

The light of His love illumines our way
As we travel life's rocky road,
Guiding us along night and day,
Giving strength to carry the heavy load.

He sent the brightest light of all
When the world was in darkness and sin,
To save mankind from his worst downfall,
And his salvation to win.

Jesus is that wonderful light
And shines in our lives today,
Removing darkness, improving our sight,
Leading us every step of the way.

# There Is Hope in Christ

Life is not always easy.
And we get discouraged sometime,
But there is something we can depend on
To bring us peace of mind.

And will help us rise above
All the heartaches and strife;
Bringing contentment to our souls,
It is the hope we have in Christ.

The trials of life crash down on us
And we are at the end of our rope,
We must take courage in His promises,
Because in Christ there is hope!

There is hope for today and tomorrow
He shares His endless wealth
And tells us in His holy word
There is hope, even after death.

That if we faithfully believe in Him
Our souls shall never die.
He gives us the eternal hope
That we shall live with Him on high!

## Brotherhood

There is a paradox in the way we act;
Hard for many to face the real facts.
They act one way and really feel another
When it comes to acting as sisters and brothers.

It is somewhat difficult for us to get past
The barriers of social position and class.
We should put forth an effort to start
Looking beyond the surface and into the heart.

And see that everyone is God's very own
He will receive each of us in His heavenly home.
A little soul searching would do each of us good.
It would help bring about true brotherhood.

# A Recipe for Successful Living

These special fruits of the spirit
That I have whipped together;
Will give you all the strength you need
To brave life's stormy weather!

Use two and one-half cups of patience,
And one and one-half cups of love.
One-half cup each of goodness and joy
Rolled in blessings from God above.

Add three-fourths cup of kindness,
One cup each of self-control and peace.
Throw in a dash of forgiveness and gentleness
To make sure all malice and hatred cease.

Mix all these ingredients well.
Let your heart be the mixing bowl.
You'll have enough for an entire lifetime
To strengthen and nourish the soul.

This recipe will serve all mankind
As you season it with faith and prayer.
Nothing can ever come your way
That you will not be able to bear.

# HOLIDAYS

# Remembering Christmases of Long Ago

The hustle and bustle began weeks before.
Preparations varied . . . washing windows . . .
  scrubbing the floors.
Everything had to be spic and span . . .
  glistening and bright . . . not a speck
  of dirt in sight!

Mama, adorned in an apron made of
  bleached flour sack . . . with flour on
  the tip of her nose . . . was busy baking
  layers and layers of cakes . . . smiling . . .
  as she hummed her favorite Christmas carol.

She made so many of them . . . coconut,
  fruit, chocolate, pineapple, and pound,
  some square and some round.

The delicious aroma spread throughout the house
Little brother and I tipped around as quietly
  as a mouse.
Mama said we couldn't frolic at all . . .
  because it would make her cake fall.

We stood patiently in line waiting to lick
  the batter bowl.
To be first was my primary goal.
But little brother nudged me with his
  elbow . . . letting me know he was going
  to be first. No contest there . . . I always gave in.

Homemade decorations were finished . . .
    just waiting to trim the tree when the
    older brothers fetched it from the woods.
They always found the most beautiful
    cedar tree . . . branches full and green.
The fresh forest smell added to the festive
    odors of Christmas as well.

Soon it's Christmas Eve . . . the excitement
    mounts.
There is chatter and laughter throughout
    The quaint old farmhouse.

The day goes by fast . . . it gets dark
    at last.
All the children must go to bed early, we
    are told.
No one can be awake when jolly old
St. Nick slides down the chimney . . .
    making his long-awaited entrance!

Each one of us puts our shoe box in a
    special place to receive our Christmas
    goodies . . . and race off to bed . . .
    filled with so much joy!
Oh boy . . . tomorrow would be the big
    day . . . Christmas Day!

Almost breathless . . . I lie very still . . .
    covers over my head . . . so afraid.
When Santa Claus came I wanted to be sleeping
Because my sister said he'd put ashes in my
    eyes if he caught me peeping.

It was a long, long uncomfortable night.
At last . . . it was daylight . . . finally morning
   comes . . . Christmas morning at last!

We hop out of bed . . .
   Rush to our shoe boxes and find . . .
   fruits, nuts and candies of different kinds.
Sometimes a small toy . . . like a horn
   or harmonica . . . or perhaps a scooter
   would be found . . . to be shared
   by all the children.

Although we didn't have a lot of gifts,
   that was the best day of the year.
The gift that was better than any
   material thing . . . was the love we
   shared together . . .
And I wanted that day to last forever!

## The Greatest Gift

The world was without a Savior,
They were in darkness and had lost their way
God sent His Son Jesus, the greatest gift
To bring hope on that Christmas Day.

They had waited years for His coming
To spread His light upon the earth.
Joy filled their hearts with songs of praise
When they heard the news of the holy birth.

The shepherds watching their flocks rejoiced,
As they heard the heavenly angels sing
Glory to God in the highest and on earth
For the gift of the newborn King!

Wise men from the East traveled far.
The bright star guided them on their way.
They brought gifts for the newborn babe,
But none matched the Gift born on that day.

## Follow the Star

On that cold wintry December night
The star over Bethlehem was shining bright;
Guiding the Wise Men on their way
To the lowly manger their homage to pay.

They had heard of the newborn King,
And of the joy and love He would bring.
The peace and good will to all mankind.
This holy place they were anxious to find.

The star of Bethlehem still shines today.
And we must follow it to find our way
To Jesus Christ our Savior and Lord,
And receive salvation as our reward.

## A Christian Journey through the New Year

In the month of January
Let us not be weary
Of the year's tasks we have to face.
God will give us guidance and grace.

February is the month of love.
Show it to your neighbors and God above,
Give it freely, expecting nothing in return.
Deep down in your heart, let it burn.

March, the month that spring marches in.
Let's do some spring cleaning; clean out sin.
An excellent way to make a start
Is to dust the cobwebs of hate from your heart.

April is the month of showers
Let's shower kindness through all the hours.
Even be kind when one is not deserving;
It will show God's love; the One that you are serving.

The month of beautiful flowers is May.
Let us send flowers, a good way to say
Just how much you love your mother,
Or the love you have for one another.

June is the romantic month of weddings,
And new highways couples will be treading.
A beautiful girl with the groom by her side;
Representing Christ with the church as His bride.

In July we'll let freedom ring.
Let every living soul pray and sing
Songs of praises for the freedom Christ gave
When He died on the cross for our souls to save.

August, the last full month for frolic and fun.
A time to wind up activities begun.
Let's remember our times with family and friends.
Relinquish the dread that summer is coming to an end.

In September we pause for a rest.
For some, this special day is the best.
While resting, remember Christ did the same,
And whatever you do should be done in His name.

October, the month of jokes and funny faces;
A lot of fun if kept in the proper places.
Don't be guilty of adding a trick to a treat
That you give to some innocent child to eat.

The turkey month is November.
Let us be sure that we remember
To thank God for all His blessings,
Including the turkey and all the dressing.

December is the best month in the year,
Because God gave us a gift that is so dear,
So enjoy Christmas; every precious minute,
But for heaven's sake, leave Christ in it!

## A New Year's Prayer

Lord, as the old year fades into the new,
I turn all my inner thoughts to You.
Kindly asking for mercy and love,
That only You can send from above.

Give me guidance and hope through the coming year.
When faced with something that may cause me fear,
May Your wisdom lead me in the right direction;
Extend Your strong arms for my protection . . .

Against all the pitfalls I may have to face
As I continue running this life's race.
Please give me Your understanding and forgiveness
When I bow before You and humbly confess . . .

All the sins and wrongs I have done.
Lead me to make peace with everyone.
Erase every little bitterness from my heart
Let the year get off to a good start.

And Lord, should my faith become a bit weak,
Your strength and mercy I prayerfully seek.
To take away all the anxiety and fear
That may come my way throughout the New Year!


## A New Year's Wish to Loved Ones

As the old year comes to a close
And time ushers in the new,
May all the hopes and dreams you have
Be fulfilled and come true.

May you take time to love,
For love is the essence of your soul.
May you take time to forgive,
And to no past regrets hold.

May all the time you spend be fruitful
In carrying out the Master's plans;
Enhancing love, peace, and kindness,
Giving service to your fellowman.

May your joys be many,
And your sorrows few,
As you sail upon the sea of time
The whole New Year through.

# The Man and His Dream

Martin Luther King,
　　Worthy of the name.
Because of his dream
　　He will be remembered
　　Through the ages
　　On the pages
　　Of history
And in the hearts
　　Of the citizens of the world.

Martin Luther King,
　　A man consumed with passion
　　To change the course of history
　　And the courage to pursue it;
Who dared to dream of a better life
　　For all mankind.
His wisdom, vision and faith
　　Were put into action
　　To fulfill his dream.

Martin Luther King,
　　Didn't see the world
　　In black and white
But only what was right
　　In God's sight,
For all humanity the world over.

Martin Luther King,
    Faced the arrows and slings
    Of prejudice and hate
    Verbal and physical abuse,
    But kept his eyes on the prize,
His dream that all God's children
    Could be free
Regardless of race, color, or creed.

Martin Luther King,
    A man with a dream
    Of seeing all colors
    Sitting down
Together as one big family,
    God's family . . .
Free from discrimination and hate,
    Before it was too late!

Martin Luther King,
    Worked tirelessly on his dream,
    Facing persecution, prison walls
    But stood tall
    Fighting harder for justice
    And equality for all.

Martin Luther King,
    His nonviolence was tested many times,
    He was big in action,
    But humble in heart;
Always on the front line,
    A drum major for justice
    Fighting to do his part
    To let freedom ring!

Martin Luther King,
  Struggled not to be stopped,
  He went to the mountain top,
  Had a view of the promised land
  And the future
  Seeing all God's children
  Being free at last,
  Free at last!

Martin Luther King,
  Went through a lot of strife.
  An assassin's bullet took his life
  It killed his body,
But his spirit still lives and leads us
  And the dream lives on
  In the hearts of every
  God-fearing citizen of the world
  Nothing can take away the glory!

Martin Luther King's
  Dream must never die
      The man stood tall
      For us all
He paid the ultimate price
      With his life
      For his dream!

# The Tragedy and Triumph of the Cross

It makes my heart sad when I think of the cross
That they hung my Savior on.
He suffered and died in our behalf,
Although He had done no wrong.

It was an ugly old cross that He had to carry;
Then they nailed His hands and feet.
And placed a crown of thorns upon His head,
Making the dreadful ordeal complete.

He went through all the agony and pain;
Suffered and died for you and me.
Never opening His mouth to say a mumbling word,
And set a world of sinners free.

Dying on that old rugged cross was such a tragedy,
But the triumph came on the third day,
When Christ our Savior rose from the grave
And washed all our sins away.

A cross today is no longer a tragedy.
It is a symbol of everlasting love.
The horizontal bar points to our fellowman,
And the vertical bar to God up above.

It also represents Christ's triumph over sin and death.
And no longer makes me feel sad,
Because I know all power is in His hands.
He's the best friend we ever had.

182

## Signed, Sealed, and Delivered

Our salvation was signed
With Christ's precious blood.
He went through all the suffering,
Tumult and flood,
When He took our place
And died upon the cross
Making it possible
That our souls would not be lost.

Our salvation was sealed
When they closed the tomb.
Man would no longer
Have to face darkness and doom.
His mission was completed
To free us from death and sin.
His love and tender mercy
Had brought it to an end.

Our salvation was delivered
When He rose from the grave.
He had kept His promise
Of our soul to save.
Stepped out on earth
Declaring all power was in His hands,
And sent the Holy Spirit,
By our side to always stand.

## His Precious Blood

Jesus shed His blood for me,
Just to make a sinner free.
Had He not gone to the cross
Then my soul would be lost.

No greater love can anyone give
To suffer and die that I might live.
And now I live for Him each day,
Striving to show others the way . . .

To be worthy of the debt He paid,
And the loving sacrifice that He made.
Showing His kind mercy and grace,
Shedding His precious blood in my place.


## What Is a Mother?

She is a lot of persons
All wrapped up in one,
And it is so amazing
How she gets everything done!

She's a babysitter and wife,
And the number one chef and cook,
A maid who washes, irons, and cleans
Every cranny, corner, and nook.

A good dietitian she has to be
So that everyone is satisfied .
Making sure there are no complaints
About how something is baked or fried.

She becomes a referee and legal advisor
Whenever the children have a fight.
Everybody always looks to her
To make everything right.

She takes on the role of doctor and nurse.
Tries hard to keep everybody well.
Always overlooking the possibility
That she could come down with a sick spell.

A little psychiatry and psychology are practiced
As she strives to figure out
The weird behavior of some family member,
But finds that's something she knows little about.

She is back and forth as a taxi driver
Hauling the kids to school and athletic meets.
Business manager and errand runner;
Shopping for the best foods to eat.

She's a repair person, gardener, and seamstress,
Tutor, teacher, religious leader,
Keeping everybody's schedule straight,
Filling in wherever they need her.

In addition, she may hold down a full-time job
While being a wife, mother, lover and friend.
It's the regular routine of being a mother.
Her diversified jobs never come to an end.

She keeps the family together
Whenever the times get rough;
Works steadily just like a hired hand,
But could never be paid enough . . .

For all her years of service
And for all the love she gives
The family is indebted to her
As long as she shall live.

Now what a mother really is . . .
It will take too long to say,
Why not just give her honor and praise
On this her special day!

## I Owe You, Mom

Nine months you nourished and gave me a start
In a warm place inside close to your heart.
Fondly cuddling and waiting for the happy day
When you'd give birth and start me on my way.

Then through the pain you gave me life
And have stood by me through all the strife.
When life was hard for me to understand
You were always there to give a helping hand.

Reflecting back on my life today,
There is no way I could ever pay
For all the things you have done for me;
Without you, Mom, I wouldn't be . . .

The type of person that I am now
You helped to make it possible somehow.
By steering my life in the right direction
And was always there for my protection.

Everyday of my life I give you the praise
For helping me in so many ways
And especially on this day I give to you
My love and thanks for all that you do.


## A Mother's Love

Next to God's love
    Is that of a mother's.
Through her suffering
    A child is born,
        It grows
            And learns
Under her loving guidance and care.

When her child hurts
    She feels the pain
And with a simple touch
    She makes it go away.

She neglects herself
    And makes concessions everyday.

Her words of compassion
  Make fears vanish like dark clouds
  When the sun bursts through.
And tears are dried up like
  The midmorning dew.

Her kind words, like rays of sunshine
  Melt the frosts of discouragement
  And disappointments.

When her child goes wrong
  She is filled with pain,
But willingly forgives and realizes
  Into each life falls a bit of rain.
  She starts all over again.

Her love is so strong and flexible
  It stretches and stretches
To include all of life's twists and turns.
  It is a wellspring
    That overflows.
The more she gives, the more it grows.

Her voice is wrapped up in love
  Which is as pleasant as a bird
    Singing on a spring morning.
      So pleasing to hear,
  Like music to the ear.

Her child may be reckless and wild
  Still, her love is so Christlike
Because she'd give her life
  For her child!

Many loves come and go,
    Lovers, sisters, brothers,
But thank God
    For the love of mothers!

## A Mother's Plea

My son, my son,
How can I get through to you?
All I ever wanted was to help you see it through
All of life's toils, struggles and fears,
I shared each one through all the years.

There were times when it was impossible
For me to be there.
But that never meant that I didn't care
About what was going on in your life;
And deeply concerned about all your strife.

The past is behind us,
We should now look ahead.
Forget about the bad times, remember the joys instead.
There is a lot of love I want to share with you.
Just give me a chance and we can start anew.

We can have the kind of love
Between a mother and son,
That I've always wanted, before my life is done.
So let us share our joys, our love and sorrows,
And look forward to a lot of beautiful tomorrows.

It is never too late
To make a new start
If you have love and forgiveness in your heart,
You may find it hard to understand my point of view,
But just give it a try and God will see you through.


## Remembering on Memorial Day

Sometimes it is not enough
Just to remember on this day
Our heroes of yesteryear
Who have passed away.

They bravely fought in battle.
For their country they gave their lives,
Never returning to their homeland
Leaving parents, children, and wives.

We take for granted the price they paid
And think more of frolic and fun on this day
We should pause and take serious thought
About what they actually had to pay.

They gave all they had for you and me;
We gave nothing in return.
No greater love can anyone give,
This fact we should all learn.

So pause and say a prayer of thanks,
Pray for the families they left behind.
They gave their lives to make us safe
And to give us peace of mind.

# The Father Figure

There is a little problem
In our society.
Leaving fathers out
Is a noticeable tendency.

When an engagement is announced
There is a picture of the bride.
But we seldom see
Who will be walking by her side.

There is another picture of the bride
When the wedding ends.
The poor groom is not in sight;
Him, this should offend.

He is an important part
Of this marriage union.
It's somewhat like leaving
Christ out of our Holy Communion.

When the first child comes
The happy news will tell;
Both, mother and child
Are doing well.

And here, we see again
They have left out the father.
Telling about his conditions
No one ever cares to bother!

A father is an important part
Of the family scene
Because he provides
One-half of the child's genes.

He is head of the family
And should always be there
To help train, mold, and guide
All the children with care.

A father is not
Just a figure of the mind.
He is one who is understanding,
Always loving and kind.

He stresses the values
Of Christian living;
Imparting strength and knowledge
And his love always giving.

He has the wisdom and foresight
And the courage to lead.
Works hard to provide
All the family needs.

He is more than a father,
He is also a friend.
Whenever there is a problem
On him they can depend.

He serves as a role model;
Especially for his sons.
With his strong morals
Makes sure that this is done.

He wants his sons
To grow up and be like him
So the light of his shining character
Never grows dim.

When he's faced with burdens
And carrying a heavy load;
He may find himself straying
From the straight and narrow road.

A good question to ask himself
Will always be . . .
"Do I want my sons to grow up,
And be just like me?"

So on this special day, fathers
We give our love and praise
And pray for your strength
Throughout the rest of your days . . .

That God, our heavenly Father
Will show His mercy and grace,
And in the family unit,
You will keep your rightful place!

## You Changed My Life

I never want to think about
How life would be without you, Dad.
In my heart there is no doubt
You're the best dad I could have had.

You've always been there for me
To help when I most needed you.
When things got rough you helped me to see
How I could make it through.

You changed the course of my entire life;
Standing by me through thick and thin
Giving guidance and courage through all the strife
Assuring me I could always win.

## All My Love, Daddy

This is just a special day
That has been set aside
To recognize all the dads;
I do it now with pride.

Because you are the very best
In every possible way
So it makes it extremely easy
To give you all my love today.

And every day that follows
For as long as we shall live.
Every day is Father's Day,
Because of all the love you give.

194

## Thoughts of Freedom on Independence Day

As our thoughts go inward on this day,
We begin to think of the price we pay
To live and prosper in this great land,
Sometimes it is hard to understand.

It's called the land of the free and home of the brave;
Yet there are many still living as slaves!
Not in bondage with a ball and chain,
But a lack of freedom to choose, is very plain.

To choose where we live, are we completely free?
Without being hindered by those who don't agree
That everyone is entitled to the best in life,
And should not have to go through all the strife.

There are many other inequities some have to face
Forcing them to stay in their "proper" place.
Why must their freedom have a different price tag?
Makes one realize real freedom is just a gag!

## Real Freedom

We enjoy our freedom
In this great land,
And are thankful to those
Who proudly took a stand.

To fight for this country
That we might be free,
To live, grow and love
In peace and liberty.

But the only real freedom
That will ever last
Is the freedom that was won for us
A long time in the past.

When Christ our heavenly Father
Willingly died upon the cross;
To free us from all our sins
So our souls would not be lost.

He gave something to us
That man can never give;
Salvation and eternal life,
With Him in heaven to live.

# A Pause That Is Restful

This Labor Day we pause to honor
The working force of this land;
Those who struggle everyday
For themselves and their fellowman.

We remember Christ paused to take a rest
When He created the world;
Looked upon everything and said it was good;
Including the sun, moon, and stars He'd hurled.

As we enjoy our rest today
And reflect upon all that we have done
We realize that we also labor
For our Master, the Holy One.

When we have finished our labor for Him
And go home to our heavenly rest,
There is no comparison of what we feel today
Because there with Him will be the best!

# The First Thanksgiving

The first Thanksgiving came from the heart,
When the white man and Indian both took a part
In thanking God for supplying their needs.
No one thought of race, color or creed.

One had helped the other to survive.
It was God's divine way of keeping them alive.
That they may prosper and multiply in this new land,
And learn to love and respect their fellowman.

They dined together and were filled with laughter,
But history tells us what happened thereafter.
They fought over the land; there was utter devastation,
The Indians were herded together on a reservation.

If we could go back to that Thanksgiving of old,
And all races came together for one common goal;
To join in praising God for supplying our needs,
Forgetting about race, color, or creed.

Feasting and rejoicing as God's big family,
Words can't describe how wonderful that would be.
As all joined together to meditate and pray;
That would really be a genuine Thanksgiving Day!

# Thank Thee, Lord

For the food we eat
And the clothes we wear,
For the shelter over our heads
And the joys we share
    We thank Thee, Lord.

For eyes to see
And ears to hear,
For family and friends
We love so dear
    We thank Thee, Lord.

For the freedoms you give
And Your understanding heart.
For all of our successes
Of which you are a part,
    We thank Thee, Lord.

May what we feel
On this Thanksgiving Day,
Last now and forever.
And may we continue to say,
    We thank Thee, Lord.

## ABOUT THE BOOK

Julia Neal Sykes began writing poetry in her sixties when the death of her husband from cancer and the killing of her seventeen-year-old cat by dogs left her grief stricken and lonely.

Yet these are not depressing verses; on the contrary, they are full of faith and love, courage and the appreciation of life and its beauty. These deaths gave her a new perspective and she began to treasure much that she had taken for granted.

One of the very first poems, "Ode to Fluffy," won an honorable mention in a poetry contest and since then her poems have been published in: *"Golden Treasury of "Great Poems",* by "World of Poetry Press", 2431 Stockton Boulevard, Sacramento, CA 95817, and in *"Love's Greatest Treasury, Vol. II",* by the "American Poetry Association," 250 A Potrero Street, P.O. Box 1803, Santa Cruz, CA 95061-1803. Her poems have also appeared in *New Voices in American Poetry.*

In 1997, she co-authored a book entitled "Footprints on the Rough Side of the Mountain". An African-American niche in the history of a Southern textile city, reflecting life in the years 1895 – 1995.

Kamkyi Books is proud to publish this revised edition of the works of author Julia Neal Sykes.